THE VICTORY ERA

in Color!

By Jeff Ethell

America showed her proudest colors during the 1940s, as these rare photos attest.

Contents

Publisher: Roy J. Reiman
Editor: Mike Beno
Assistant Editors: Kristine Krueger, Henry de Fiebre
Art Director: Gail Engeldahl
Art Associate: Julie Wagner
Production Assistants: Ellen Lloyd, Judy Pope
Photo Coordination: Trudi Bellin

©1994, Jeffrey L. Ethell

Reiman Publications, L.P.
5400 S. 60th St., Greendale WI 53129

Reminisce Books
International Standard Book Number: 0-89821-127-1
Library of Congress Catalog Number: 94-67301
All rights reserved.
Printed in U.S.A.
Cover and back cover photos: National Archives

MOM AND DAD. Captain Erv Ethell posed on his P-51D Mustang, carrying the likeness of his wife. When son Jeff gazed at his parents through this vivid window in time, he was captivated. The inspiration led him to track down the largest collection of 1940s color in the world.

INTRODUCTION

By Jeff Ethell

World War II must have been fought in black and white…at least to judge by the photos Americans have seen for the past 50 years.

Newsreel footage and history books have trained the postwar generation to think of the 20th century's pivotal event in shades of gray. That's too bad, because according to those who were there, the tanks, jeeps, aircraft and people in that war were the most colorful in history. The rare color photographs you'll see in this book offer proof of that.

My own impressions of the Second World War were molded by my father's Army Air Forces scrapbook. The photos he took in North Africa gave me a glimpse at the P-38s he and his friends flew while fighting a war far from home. When I was a youngster during the 1950s, I'd spend *hours* poring over those black-and-white glimpses into Dad's youth.

I found myself wondering what those black-and-white images would have looked like in real color. This interest was kindled by a single color slide (above).

Captain Erv Ethell, 39th Fighter Squadron, was sitting on the wing of his P-51D Mustang. Spread across the nose was my mother's name, with her portrait below.

I was around 10 years old when I first found this shot. Was that steely-eyed fighter pilot in the leather helmet really my dad? You mean World War II actually *was* fought in color? Dad had no idea where he'd gotten the slide, since he used black-and-white film. He must have grown tired of my badgering him about it.

Colorful Search Begins

I continued to look at that slide across the years, and as I started a career of writing books about aviation and World War II, I wanted to believe there was more vintage color to be found. But where was it?

During my first 10 years of book writing, I came to assume there wasn't much color out there. But every now and then a stray slide or two would show up, shared by a veteran from his personal photo collection. This teased me to dig deeper.

Strictly on a hunch, I started to ask for color photos ♂→

whenever I wrote letters to veterans requesting information. This cracked the tap to a dribble, and a few dozen incredibly beautiful slides started to trickle in, mostly from personal collections.

It was always the same—a pilot here or a soldier there would have a few slides, never more than 10 or so, but they were something to see. I'd project them up on the wall and bask in the past coming alive.

Though it seemed impossible, I started to hatch the idea of a book made up of nothing but color photography from the World War II era. Historians told me that color images of those days just didn't exist.

I put increasing amounts of my own time and money into the quest for vintage color by writing more letters and making phone calls—mostly getting nowhere. I began to think maybe they were right.

Became an Adventure

Little by little, the slides kept dribbling in. This was maddening, since I had a gut feeling there had to be a waterfall dammed up behind this steadily dripping faucet. I felt as if I were onto an Indiana Jones adventure, and kept on digging.

Since color photography obviously did exist in the 1940s, I called the inventors of color film, Eastman Kodak Company in Rochester, New York. I was surprised to learn they had but one or two wartime color images in their entire archive.

That seemed impossible! But when I was put through to Phil Condax, senior curator, the story behind early color film unfolded.

In 1935, Eastman Kodak announced an entirely new 16mm movie film called Kodachrome. In September 1936, Kodachrome was made available in roll film, 35mm (18 exposures) and 828 (8 exposures, 28mm wide). It was sold with the amateur market in mind.

Therein lie the seeds for the scarcity of World War II color pictures in magazines and museum files. The pro photographers of the day used sheet film, 4" x 5" or larger, and considered the 35mm format a toy for the family snapshot taker.

By the early '40s, this technology had reached the hands of many enthusiastic amateurs and a few professionals who would soon be at war around the world with their rugged new cameras and color slide film. Without knowing it, they'd become a small band of unheralded historians.

During the 1940s, Kodachrome was for sale, in apparently significant quantities, in camera shops and drugstores. Its original 10 ASA film speed was considerably slower than most black-and-white film, but still fast enough to take short exposure snapshots in good light.

"I wanted to shoot for the future, to create a record of what I was seeing…"

One big inconvenience facing users of this new film was processing. According to Condax, by the time World War II started, Kodachrome was available in professional sheet film sizes, but Kodak's Rochester plant was the sole facility able to develop the film.

During many of the multiple processing steps, temperatures could not vary by more than plus or minus 1/10th of a degree. War photographers wanted their results instantly, so anything that couldn't be developed in a makeshift field darkroom was unacceptable.

What's more, Kodachrome was so sensitive to heat it couldn't be carted around in the field without concern. Most professionals couldn't live with that…but amateurs didn't give it a second thought.

Found a Colorful Veteran

My quest for color finally led me to 55th Fighter Group enlisted man Bob Sand in Bellingham, Washington. When I met Bob, the dam finally burst.

Bob went to war in England as a P-38 propeller specialist and P-51 crew chief. Arriving in 1943, he was so impressed with the rich, deep colors of the countryside that he wrote his parents, Oscar and Rosa Sand, asking them to send color film and a camera to shoot it. He wanted to capture what he was seeing.

Oscar crisscrossed their hometown until he found a camera store that sold Kodak Bantams from $125 down to $37…Oscar bought the cheapest one and sent it off to Bob.

A few weeks later, Oscar found two rolls of 828 Kodachrome and shipped them to England. Every few weeks for the duration, Bob would receive one or two rolls of Kodachrome from his dad or friends.

Bob wrote his parents on Thanksgiving 1943, "I've shot up one roll of film, and while this roll contains nothing spectacular, I hope it is the beginning of something that may have a little interest later on." By the end of the war, Bob Sand had captured life on a wartime fighter base with over 430 full-color slides. He did it without the aid of a light meter or fancy equipment.

After finding Bob, I knew a color picture book was possible, but he was understandably gun-shy at loaning his treasure to a total stranger. He'd carefully archived the slides in glass mounts for over 45 years, storing them in wooden boxes away from climatic changes.

Treasure Trove Shared

It took me 6 months to convince him to let me see them while we built a mutual relationship of trust based on our love of history. He knew what he had must be shared for posterity, so I wore him down until he relented. When I received his originals, removed them from the tiny wooden boxes and carefully viewed them, it felt as if I'd uncovered a treasure.

Meanwhile, my hundreds of letters to veterans began to bear fruit. The next mother lode came through Bob Kuhnert, 355th Fighter Group, who was in contact with Alexander "Cal" Sloan of Green Bay, Wisconsin, another enlisted man in love with photography.

Cal grew up with an artistic bent. Armed with a Zeiss Contax 35mm camera, one of the finest of the late '30s, Cal quickly established himself as a budding professional photographer.

With World War II upon him, Cal enlisted and shipped out to England with the 1066th Signal Company, then had his wife, Gertrude, send the Contax over. She bought what Kodachrome she could find in drugstores, one or two rolls at a time. Cal ended up with more than 200 images, each shot with careful precision using a Weston light meter.

"I had an eye for this," he recalls. "I wanted to shoot for the future, to create a record of what I was seeing." Cal sent me his originals without hesitation. Opening his box of slides was another archaeological experience.

Bill Skinner of Boonton, New Jersey worked for a camera store in 1938 when he got his first Kodak Bantam for $25. By the time he was flying Spitfires with the 31st Fighter Group in North Africa, Sicily and Italy, his mother had sent him a Bantam Special. When she could find it, she bought Kodachrome and shipped it off to him four or five rolls at a time.

Bill sent it home undeveloped with men rotating back to the States, so he didn't see the results until he returned himself. The slides surprised him. "If I'd known how good I was doing, I'd have taken more!"

His color record of life in the mud, sweat and sand of the Mediterranean looks as good today as it did then.

Fred Bamberger, Tamarac, Florida, discovered 35mm color for his Contax in 1936 when he was already being paid to shoot photos for Acme News Pictures. His shots of the Hindenburg disaster established his niche.

After joining the Army, he went through the service's

AUTHOR JEFF ETHELL poses with World War II vintage fighter plane like his father's (page 5). Jeff is an aviation and military historian who's written more than 50 books on the subjects.

first photo school for officers, became the base photo officer at Randolph Field, then went overseas with Colonel Elliot Roosevelt's 90th Photo Recon Wing.

Serving as photo officer for the 12th Air Force in Italy, Fred had an unlimited pass to take his personal camera everywhere. He shot close to 1,500 color slides in his off-duty hours! I was dumbfounded during my first visit with Fred as we spent *hours* watching his slides.

A most exciting discovery was thousands of wartime color transparencies in the National Archives. Some of these pictures were well known, but I had a hunch there were more.

Through the generous permission of Betty Hill, chief of the Still Picture Branch, I began to dig with fellow historian Stan Piet and my daughter, Jennie. In a short time, hundreds of transparencies, misfiled in the wrong years, began to turn up. With the help of Archives research assistant Dale Connelly, we uncovered color photos virtually hidden for decades. Many of these historic pictures are shown here for the first time.

A True Look at the Past

The images these historians and veterans have shared for this book are real, just as they were taken by the soldiers, sailors, marines and airmen in the middle of it all. These pictures have not been colorized by Ted Turner...there are no re-enactors dressed in period uniforms with props gathered from museums.

Their value to history is almost immeasurable, and the impact of finding the only known color images of this historic era was overwhelming to me.

In this collection are photos of the famed all-black 332nd Fighter Group, which fought the Germans and segregation...Bob Hope and Frances Langford entertaining the troops in 1943...FDR, Churchill and Stalin at Yalta...Mt. Vesuvius erupting in 1944...Women Airforce Service Pilots...and most all of it comes courtesy of the veterans *who were there.*

That these veterans trusted me to share their pictures in this book is an honor...and I hope it will change the perceptions of many. Please sit back and enjoy this rare color trip into the World War II years, the era of victory.

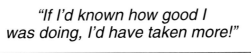

"If I'd known how good I was doing, I'd have taken more!"

CHAPTER ONE

ON THE HOME FRONT

World War II unified Americans as nothing before or since. With few exceptions, people put themselves behind the war effort at home in order to give our soldiers, sailors and airmen not only better equipment, but more of it.

Most historians agree that the single most important factor in the Allied victory was America's massive production effort. As one Army Air Forces downed pilot told his Luftwaffe interrogator before being shipped off to POW camp, "No nation on earth can beat Henry Ford and General Motors."

There was no more dramatic example of the U.S. production miracle than the manufacture of aircraft. In 1939, as Europe went to war, America was woefully under-equipped with a few thousand obsolescent airplanes.

In 1940, President Roosevelt was fully aware of the nation's ill-preparedness, and called for industry to produce 50,000 planes a year and train 100,000 crews to fly them. Some Americans rallied to his call, but not until the bombing of Pearl Harbor did they jump in with angered determination.

The Numbers Tell All

From July 1940 to August '45, the U.S. built 299,293 aircraft, 802,161 engines and untold millions of spare parts. By comparison, Britain built 128,835 planes between 1939 and 1945, while our enemies Japan and Germany built 58,834 and 113,514, respectively. Tank production mirrors the same results: the U.S. built 60,973, compared to 23,202 in Britain, 19,926 in Germany and 2,464 in Japan.

By the end of 1943, there were 18.7 million more people at work in the U.S. than in 1939, and they were producing 40% of the world's armaments by the beginning of 1944. World War II emphatically ended the Depression.

In March 1944 alone, Americans produced 9,113 aircraft. In 1944, Henry J. Kaiser was producing one Liberty Ship a day and Henry Ford was building one B-24 Liberator four-engine bomber every hour at his Willow Run plant.

Socially, America changed forever when women took their place in the work force, never to be pushed out again. Had it not been for this infusion of enthusiastic and skilled labor, the war would have been far more difficult to win.

"Rosie the Riveter", with her hair tied up in a bandanna, became famous as the symbol of mothers, wives and girlfriends building planes for their sons and sweethearts off to war.

Heroes at Home

In the end, Hitler and Tojo could not withstand the industrial might of the American worker who shouldered so much of the responsibility for winning World War II.

By the time it was over, the U.S. had spent $288 billion—far more than any other nation—to make victory possible. Admiral Isoroku Yamamoto, who had gone to school at Harvard, reluctantly planned the Pearl Harbor attack after pleading with his government not to start a war with an underestimated America.

Upon receiving the first reports of the spectacular devastation his carrier planes had wreaked upon Hawaii, he sat back and soberly told his officers, "I fear all we have done is awaken a sleeping giant and fill him with a terrible resolve." How right he was.

AUTOS TO AIRPLANES. Hudson Motor Car Company did what every other private firm in the nation was ordered to do...change over to war production. These women at Hudson are working on an airplane wing panel before it's shipped off to the factory for assembly. Most war production was spread across the continent, speeding the process and eventually overwhelming the Axis.

FLYING TIGER ACE R.T. Smith (above) and his wife, Barbie (left), made a stunning couple at home both before and after he returned from flying in China. R.T.'s new Army Air Forces "pinks and greens" uniform carries not only the American silver wings on his left but, on the right, the Chinese Air Force wings he earned shooting down over eight Japanese aircraft between December 1941 and July 1942. Barbie wears a flower in her hair, a 1940s fashion standard.

HOME ON LEAVE. Getting away from the grind was a serviceman's single goal. In early 1944, Private First Class Louis Raburn (right), just married to Lavyrne (alongside him), took her home to Guymon, Oklahoma, where they met Lavyrne's cousin, Coast Guardsman Paul Shields and his girlfriend. Louis shipped overseas with the 69th Division in November of '44.

JUST ONE LITTLE KISS? Mary Alice Havener patiently leans against this Lincoln Zephyr while friend Bill Mettlen tries to steal a kiss from his wife, Wilma, at a Waco, Texas city park. Jack Havener, who took this shot, and Bill were in training at Waco Army Air Field in July 1943.

WAR BRIDE Mary Alice Havener poses with Army Aviation Cadet Paul Pincus for husband Jack at the Waco, Texas swimming pool (below). In those days, two-piece bathing suits were more than daring...Mary Alice's one-piece suit with a skirt and bathing cap was just about standard for July 1943. Soon Jack and Paul would be off to advanced flying training, that much closer to going overseas.

HOT DATE! Lieutenant George Miltz and his girlfriend take some time off for a picnic in Independence, Kansas in 1944. George, known as "Ed" to his friends, was in the Army then. As soldiers shipped overseas, they prized photos like these. Snapshots, letters, perfumed keepsakes, a lock of hair...anything to link a soldier far away from home with his girl was a most valuable possession. Not long after this photograph was taken, Ed was off to combat in the Pacific.

Robert Astrella

MEMORIES OF HOME. During the early '40s, downtown Fairhope, Alabama had its population pulled away to a large extent for wartime factory work in nearby Mobile. The town became quieter as the war went on, until hardly anyone seemed to move through it on weekdays. Hometown scenes like this were what most servicemen dreamed about when they were away.

HOME FOR CHRISTMAS, Army fighter pilot R.T. Smith celebrates the holiday with his wife, Barbie, and their children. Such moments were savored in the middle of a war, particularly for R.T., who served two combat tours. The first tour was with the American Volunteer Group, the Flying Tigers; the next came in Burma with Phil Cochran's First Air Commando Group. Cochran was made famous as Flip Corkin in Milton Caniff's "Terry and the Pirates" comic strip. Toys in wartime were hard to come by, so this is a treasure trove.

Left and above: National Archives

HOLLYWOOD AT WAR. Actor Robert Cummings (third from left) takes a break with his fellow players while making a movie at Universal Pictures. Wartime Hollywood production boomed as the studios pumped out both patriotic war films and lavish entertainment spectacles to keep spirits up on the home front. There was resentment among those in the service over the lavish life-style in Southern California, but there was no debating the powerful effect films had on morale.

EMMETT KELLY gets a last-minute touch-up on his famous makeup before a performance of the Ringling Brothers and Barnum & Bailey Circus. In spite of drastic wartime shortages and rationing, the circus managed to stay on the road, bringing a steady ray of hope to people who were wondering when their sons, daughters, husbands and boyfriends were coming home.

OLD BUT RELIABLE. George Miltz posed with his trusty 1937 Pontiac during his Army tour in Independence, Kansas in 1944. When the war started, Detroit turned to building planes, tanks, jeeps and other vehicles. After the 1942 models were sold, there were no more new cars to buy for the duration. The only alternative was to keep older cars running, often on bald tires and with worn-out fan belts due to strict rubber rationing. Gasoline was scarce anyway, so not much traveling could be done.

DOWNTOWN LOS ANGELES offered plenty of excitement for servicemen on leave or just home from the war. Army signal company veteran Cal Sloan got back in 1945 and started photographing what he had dreamed of most...places to eat. Simon's Drive-In was a popular spot, offering all the American specialties men overseas pined for.

ELEGANT MOVIE PALACES like the Fox Carthay Circle in Los Angeles were quite common in the '40s, part of Hollywood's golden age. Theater owners could afford to pay for extravagant buildings when most Americans loved movies as their major form of entertainment. Cal Sloan, an impressed young man from Green Bay, Wisconsin, snapped the photo above on a night when a Deborah Kerr movie was featured.

THE BROWN DERBY was an American icon, where movie stars like Clark Gable and Rita Hayworth had their own tables. This posh restaurant symbolized the upper-class Hollywood life-style around the world. The food was always outstanding, but any soldier lucky enough to get inside did more gawking than eating.

PLAYA DEL REY, south of Los Angeles, drew plenty of people for sun and fun in the '40s. Many American girls worked in the aircraft factories that dominated the area then, so plenty of them spent their spare time on the beach. That made this stretch of sand and surf attractive to off-duty servicemen, too!

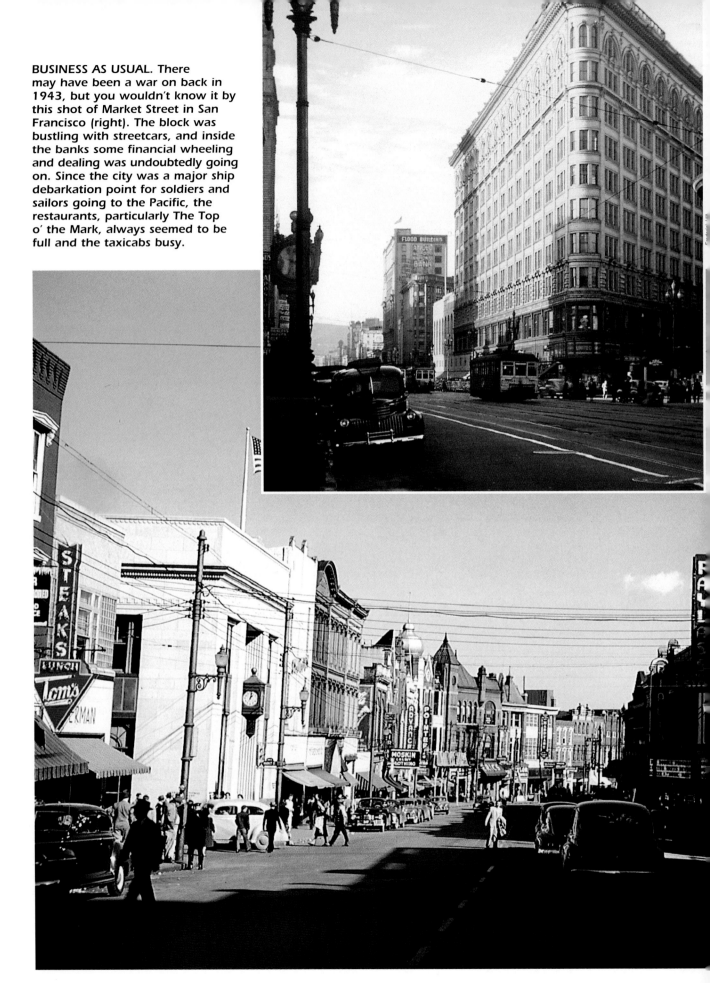

BUSINESS AS USUAL. There may have been a war on back in 1943, but you wouldn't know it by this shot of Market Street in San Francisco (right). The block was bustling with streetcars, and inside the banks some financial wheeling and dealing was undoubtedly going on. Since the city was a major ship debarkation point for soldiers and sailors going to the Pacific, the restaurants, particularly The Top o' the Mark, always seemed to be full and the taxicabs busy.

WINGS HIGH, WINGS LOW. Biplanes, a holdover from the 1930s, played a part in the American military right into the '40s, though they were used in secondary roles. These Curtiss SBC Helldivers and the Berliner-Joyce OJ-1 on the right sit on the line at St. Louis' Naval Reserve Aviation Base in July 1940. The military biplane era was more like a giant flying club due to severe isolationist budget restrictions. All that would change in a very short time.

SAILOR AND SON. Donald Amend, below, puts his boy on the wing of an N2S training biplane at the New Orleans Naval Air Station in 1944. Children grew up in the early 1940s with the military services in front of them at every turn. They wore miniature uniforms, watched Saturday movie serials like "Don Winslow of the Navy", read about the Flying Tigers in China and often had a relative fighting overseas.

MAIN STREET in Danville, Virginia offers a glimpse at what life was like in a typical town on the home front. To look at it, you'd never think it was wartime at all, with cars and people everywhere.

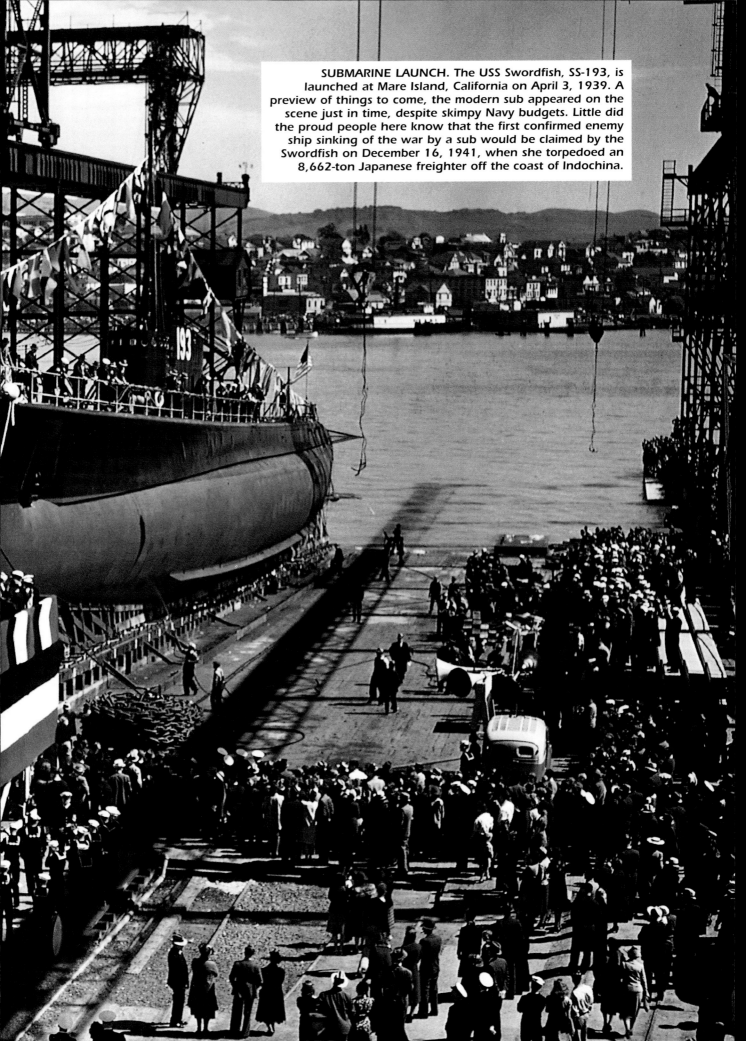

SUBMARINE LAUNCH. The USS Swordfish, SS-193, is launched at Mare Island, California on April 3, 1939. A preview of things to come, the modern sub appeared on the scene just in time, despite skimpy Navy budgets. Little did the proud people here know that the first confirmed enemy ship sinking of the war by a sub would be claimed by the Swordfish on December 16, 1941, when she torpedoed an 8,662-ton Japanese freighter off the coast of Indochina.

SKIING IN COLORADO was an ideal way for bomber pilot Bob Blair to spend a first leave in March 1943. Here wife Peggy and friend Carl Blaurock, of the Colorado Mountain Club, get the skis off the car at Loveland Pass. Bob and Peggy had been married in December 1941 before Bob shipped out for combat.

NATIONAL AIRPORT in Washington, D.C. was a bustling place in 1945 when Eastern Airlines' Great Silver Fleet of DC-3s flew up and down the East Coast. Yet things were not quite what they seemed. As in most of the private sector, with the outbreak of war the airlines were immediately commandeered by Roosevelt as critical to wartime transport of personnel and equipment. Only civilians with government clearance could travel by airliner, and pilots were made quasi-military employees called "Service Pilots" who could switch between domestic passenger flying and the Ferrying Command, which moved aircraft overseas. When the war ended, the airlines were in place for the biggest growth spurt that industry ever experienced.

FETCHING COUPLE. Lieutenant Jim Kunkle and his wife, Marian, made quite a pair in 1945 after his combat tour. Jim's wearing the "Ike Jacket" made famous when Eisenhower cut off the lower part of his uniform dress blouse for utility in the field ...the result was one of the most handsome uniforms ever created. Marian's high-heeled shoes, pillbox hat, padded shoulders and leopard-skin coat reflect high wartime fashion. Marian had two sisters who looked just as stunning...whenever Jim went out with all three, heads turned continually.

Edward Richie

Jim Kunkle

BEAUTY QUEENS made this Sumter, South Carolina town parade sparkle at the end of the war. Americans wasted no time in putting the war behind them with the same vengeance that drove home front production...and nothing quite outdid a parade in your hometown. Sumter, near Shaw Army Air Field, was a mixture of the past and the present, retaining some of its sleepy prewar nature while driven by an economy that supported the local military base. Small-town America would never be the same after World War II.

BATTLESHIP VISITS NEW YORK. The French battleship Richelieu sails from New York Harbor in November 1943, a ship without a home. When France fell to Germany, the Vichy government became collaborators while the Free French remained resistors. The Richelieu fought with Vichy until captured by the British in 1940. She sailed to the U.S. for repair and joined the British Pacific fleet, turning her guns on the Japanese. She returned to Toulon, France in August 1944.

CAMOUFLAGED BOMBER PLANT. A factory worker talks with a sailor at the Consolidated Aircraft plant in San Diego, California in July 1943. One of the Navy's largest flying boats, the four-engine PB2Y-3 Coronado in the background is in the final stages of construction before being pushed out from under the camouflage netting.

ENCASED IN ALUMINUM, workers at Consolidated put the finishing touches on the inside of a PB2Y in July of 1943. Production miracles were commonplace as people built large aircraft in record time and in record numbers. It was Henry Ford's idea of mass production gone wild as each person had a single job to do...over and over again.

PASSING INSPECTION. A woman in charge of quality control inspects a Navy PV-1 Ventura bomber at the Lockheed-Vega Plant, Burbank, California. While there were some production problems during the war, the quality of American warplanes was so high, crews had few complaints. Inspectors took their home front jobs very seriously.

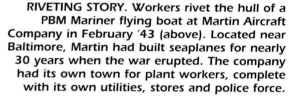

ENGINES EVERYWHERE. These women (below) assembled engines for PB4Y Liberators at Consolidated-Vultee, Downey, California. Women who'd never before worked outside the home became technically skilled and very capable during the war.

RIVETING STORY. Workers rivet the hull of a PBM Mariner flying boat at Martin Aircraft Company in February '43 (above). Located near Baltimore, Martin had built seaplanes for nearly 30 years when the war erupted. The company had its own town for plant workers, complete with its own utilities, stores and police force.

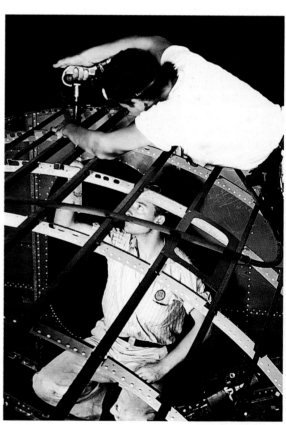

ROSIE THE RIVETER works on a PB4Y Liberator in 1943 at the Consolidated-Vultee plant, Downey, California. Rosie, really a mythical figure, became the symbol of women in war production. She seemed to be everywhere working on everything.

Thomas Doll

LONG LINE of dive-bombers seems to stretch to infinity at the Douglas Aircraft plant in El Segundo, California, 1944. These SBD-5 Dauntless dive-bombers moved on dollies fitted to tracks in the factory floor, and workers at each station did a particular job. By the time the line was shut down in July 1944, the company had produced 5,936 Dauntlesses.

BOMBER-DEARS. These women are nearly finished building a PV-1 Ventura bomber at Lockheed-Vega, Burbank. Female hands seemed to be particularly adept at working within the tight spaces associated with aircraft interiors. Women were often called on to connect fittings by sticking their arms deep into a machine and working blind, by feel.

SHE MEASURES UP. Lucille McClure of Huntington Beach, California measures for drilling on the wing of an SNV Navy basic trainer at Consolidated-Vultee in Downey, California, July 1943. In spite of the boring repetition involved with such jobs, war workers kept at it for the cause.

WAR PAINT. Pan American Airways does its bit for the war effort (below), as a Navy Air Transport Service PBM-3R Mariner flying boat is having PAA markings and the American flag painted over its military camouflage, a reflection of its being operated by a civilian company drafted into the military.

OIL CHANGE on an Army BT-13 basic trainer (above) illustrates that not only were women on the production lines and in uniform, but they worked the flight lines on military airfields across the country.

Left and above: National Archives

RAIL YARDS. Home front production, raw materials transportation and troop transport relied heavily on the American rail system, just at the end of its heyday as the country's primary means of getting from one place to another. Fast, efficient and reliable, trains could haul massive loads 24 hours a day.

Jack Havener

FORTIES FASHION. Well-dressed Betty Besse (right) and Betty Hunter (center) posed in style with their landlady, Mrs. Howard, in front of their Houston rooming house in September 1943. The house was near Ellington Field, where Army aviation cadets were training. The girlfriends and wives who followed their sweethearts around the country had hardships to contend with, but it was worth it.

National Archives

Page 30-31 photo: National Archives

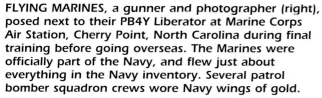

FLYING MARINES, a gunner and photographer (right), posed next to their PB4Y Liberator at Marine Corps Air Station, Cherry Point, North Carolina during final training before going overseas. The Marines were officially part of the Navy, and flew just about everything in the Navy inventory. Several patrol bomber squadron crews wore Navy wings of gold.

BOND BUYERS. War bonds were a crucial part of paying for the war effort. Without the government borrowing money from private citizens, production would have fallen drastically. In November 1944, Chicago had one of the best exhibits in the country, courtesy of the Navy, which had a strong presence in the area. From the long line shown here, the exhibit was apparently a hit.

AN OUTDOOR LOOK at the war
bond buildings on the previous page.
Chicago's Lake Michigan docks were busy
in November 1944, as the USS Wilmette, named
for a Chicago suburb, was docked for public
inspection. The area was normally used for naval
training since Lake Michigan had all the characteristics
of the ocean...except the salt. Many sailors were fully
trained and seaworthy before they ever saw an ocean.

BEACH TREATS. Florida was a fun place to visit back in 1943, despite wartime shortages. Dorothy Helen Crowder turns back to her husband, J.P., to ask what he'd like from this peanut and popcorn wagon at Daytona Beach. "Jeep", as he was known to his friends, had just come back from a tour in North Africa and Sicily, and he snapped this photo.

PAUSE THAT REFRESHES. Coca-Cola delivery men were a common sight for the WAVES during indoctrination at Northampton, Massachusetts in the summer of 1943. These men would show up to unload the all-American drink...and it never hurt to get to know a few of the female sailors in the process. Coke ended up all over the world, a welcome link with home.

Below and right: National Archives

FILL 'ER UP. Fuel trucks were busy in Kearney, California, as the Navy ran its pilots through as much training as possible before assignment to a combat unit. World War II was driven by petroleum...without it, any nation's modern war machine would grind to a halt. American oil producers had as much to do with victory as anyone, making sure the billions of gallons necessary kept flowing. When Allied bombing finally targeted German oil production and the refineries began to shut down, it was only a matter of time before it was all over.

CHAPTER TWO

IN TRAINING

Just as industry rallied to the war effort, an anemic American military shook off its prewar lethargy and trained millions to go to war… 17,955,000 to be exact. The only nation that came close to such a number was the Soviet Union.

With patriotic zeal, men and women poured from all corners of the nation to sign up, urged to duty by such memorable Victory Era slogans as "Remember Pearl Harbor", "Keep 'em Flying", and the song *Praise the Lord and Pass the Ammunition*.

The Army grew from 189,839 men in 1939 to 8,267,958 by 1945…the Navy from 125,202 to 3,380,817…the Marines from 19,432 to 474,680. The average base plus combat pay? Enlisted recruits made $71.33 a month while officers pulled in $203.50. Times certainly have changed.

Training this enormous number of men and women required an almost total conversion of the American educational system from peacetime to wartime studies.

Civilian flying schools were hired intact to train as many pilots as they could run through the doors. Colleges and universities turned entire campuses into military schools to produce officers who could lead men in the field.

Typical of this often frustrating rush, bakers became mechanics and mechanics became bakers, yet each did their best to make things work.

Cook Took Wing

One fighter pilot told the story of being sent to flight training in spite of pleading that all he wanted to do was be a cook. He reluctantly fought his war from the sky, never really understanding why he couldn't do his bit in a combat field kitchen.

In 1938, the struggling, underfunded Air Corps of 20,196 people was but 11% of the Army. Six years later, its 2,372,292 personnel made up 31% of the service.

Using 30,000 aircraft and more than a million people, the revamped Army Air Forces trained 497,433 mechanics, 347,236 gunners, 195,422 radio mechanics and operators, 193,240 pilots (another 124,000 "washed out"), 50,976 navigators and 47,354 bombardiers.

When all the figures and statistics are sorted out, two primary reasons surface for Allied victory: production and training. Hitler didn't consider placing the German economy on a war footing, and in turn didn't hire women to work in factories until 1942. By then, it was too late.

Running Out of Gas

Fuel was getting dear in Germany by 1944, as its oil refineries were being hit continually by Allied bombing. The Germans reduced training time for pilots until students with fewer than 100 hours flying experience were put up against Americans with several hundred hours of excellent Stateside flight training. The air war quickly became one-sided.

America went to war a rural, agrarian nation and emerged a global industrial and technological giant with millions of highly trained and motivated citizens who knew how to do their jobs.

Detroit was successful before World War II, but no one could have anticipated the postwar car craze born in the home front factories of the Big Three automakers. Accelerated wartime industrial production and training did more to open up the United States than any single event…nothing has been the same since.

DRESSED FOR SUCCESS. Naval aviators, each dressed differently, posed in 1942. From left to right, the pilots are wearing warm-weather khaki tropical flying gear; a Navy issue G-2 leather flying jacket and green uniform; dress whites; dress blues; and high-altitude/winter flying gear.

HIT THE BEACH! Army M4 Sherman medium tanks run out of a Navy LST (Landing Ship Tank) during a Stateside training exercise. Massive landing craft filled to the gunnels with troops and equipment came into their own during the war as the spear point for amphibious invasion in the Pacific, the Mediterranean and in Europe.

TRAINING 'CHUTERS. This jump school exercise was for U.S. Marines at Camp Pendleton, California, May 14, 1943.

National Archives

Norman Jackson

WHERE'S THE FIRE? Fire fighters (left) roll up the hoses after a drill at Ontario Army Air Base, California in early 1945.

PICTURE THIS. Photo lab technicians Zigmund Kulas and Bob Astrella stand in front of an L-4 Grasshopper at Mt. Farm, England in 1944. These men developed film from reconnaissance aircraft, an important job in modern warfare.

BUILT FOR SPEED. Test pilot Willard Boothby prepares his parachute before flying a new F4U-1 Corsair in 1942. Test pilots like Willard were thrust straight from the biplane era into flying 400-mph, 2,000-horsepower fighters. World War II was breathtaking all the way through.

NASM Arnold Collection

SCRUBBIN' UP. Pfc. Eugene Collins (left) finds everything he needs in GI issue kit...toothbrush, toothpaste, razor, shaving brush, soap and container, washcloth and towel. The tin pot helmet became everything to a soldier—tub, sink and soup bowl.

Above and right: National Archives

WHAT A MESS! Army chow (above) is recalled by private Bob Kastner, who once had to face it down during bivouac at Kelly Field, Texas. Everyone got "three squares" in the Army, even if it meant C rations in a mess kit.

REAR GUNNERS (right) were a necessity in aircraft like the SBD Dauntless dive-bomber. Nicknamed "Slow But Deadly", the SBD was vulnerable to enemy fighters, but an alert gunner could make Japanese Zero pilots think twice about closing in.

YELLOW PERIL. Primary training aircraft like these Stearman biplanes were painted bright yellow. With fledgling students at the controls, the message was clear...get out of the way!

CHEMICAL WARFARE practice at Edgewood Arsenal near Baltimore, Maryland was training of a colorful kind. The M4 Sherman medium tank was one of the Army's most successful weapons, but a gas attack could neutralize almost anything. Gas masks were standard issue to tankers and other fighting men, and chemical attack practice was a big part of Stateside training.

FORMATION FLIGHT. These Wildcats from the aircraft carrier USS Enterprise were involved in the fall 1941 practice war games. The red crosses on these planes were temporary markings for "Red Force" participants. The training came none too soon with Pearl Harbor only a month or so away. The Wildcat was the Navy's first successful single-wing fighter, even though pilots still had to crank the landing gear up by hand.

"GERONIMO!" Most every kid in World War II thought a paratrooper was supposed to say that when he jumped.

A SNAP. Student photographers practice with aerial camera.

WRENCH TURNERS (right) work on a B-17 engine. Training good mechanics took a lot of time in the '40s, since these men were true pioneers of modern technology.

COMBAT ENGINEERS of the 53rd Infantry Regiment train by moving assault boats across a body of water near Fort Ord, California, March '41.

Maurice Delay

Randy Liebermann

HOT STUFF. These men are testing the new portable M2-2 liquid oil flamethrower against a pillbox at Edgewood Arsenal, Maryland on September 23, 1944. Using tactics learned through hard Pacific island fighting, the M2-2 operator is "covered" by two infantrymen with Browning automatic rifles.

Photos: National Archives

BOOT CAMP is seldom looked on with nostalgia, particularly by those who went through notorious USMC Parris Island, South Carolina. Still, this platoon doesn't make it look so bad as they take a break in their barracks lounge on November 3, 1943.

National Archives/Stan Piet

National Archives

GUNNERY PRACTICE was training all fighter pilots and anti-aircraft gunners needed. About the only practical way to get it, though, was to shoot at "sleeves", like the red one above, towed by another airplane.

National Archives

SHINING SHOES was part of every serviceman's training—no matter which branch of service.

SIP AND STUDY. Bombardier trainees below look over their mission assignments while enjoying a Coke.

USAF

CHAPTER THREE

FROM NORTH AFRICA TO ITALY

When Winston Churchill pressed Roosevelt and Stalin for an Allied invasion of North Africa, he claimed it to be the "soft underbelly" of Europe, where the Germans and their Italian allies were supposedly ripe for defeat. It didn't go that easily.

Even without an enemy to fight, the living conditions in North Africa would have been miserable.

Soldiers slept on the ground in tents during freezing nights, refueled and maintained trucks and tanks in the blazing heat, ate poor food and tried to keep the blowing sand out of everything. The highlight of a day was often a few eggs traded from the local Berber tribesmen.

When sleeping on the ground became unbearable, soldiers dug a foxhole, stretched a pup tent over the top, stuffed in a sleeping bag and hung a "home sweet home" sign on the outside.

Water, continually in short supply, was available for drinking or brushing teeth only...except when it rained. Then there was plenty of water with the impressive by-product of boot-sucking, vehicle-swallowing mud.

The Army Air Forces in the Mediterranean Theater of Operations lived a nomadic existence in Egypt and Palestine in June 1942. Without any suitable training in the U.S., pilots were assigned ground support for the British 8th Army, which was being hard-pressed by Desert Fox Erwin Rommel's Afrika Korps.

On November 8, 1942, Operation Torch, the Allied invasion of North Africa, began under British and American naval and air support. By the end of the year, American fighter pilots came up against the Luftwaffe's best, taking terrible losses while learning the lessons of combat the hard way.

In May 1943, the Germans surrendered in Tunisia. The all-black 99th Fighter Squadron, which later joined the all-black 332nd Fighter Group, went into action.

On to Sicily

Montgomery's 8th and Patton's 7th Armies took Sicily, then invaded Italy. The Italians surrendered in September, yet Kesselring's German Army kept British and American forces at bay, stopping them cold at Anzio and demonstrating that the Germans were far from defeated.

The major prize, however, was the ability to bomb Germany from both west and south as the strategic 15th Air Force formed at bases in southern Italy.

The tactical 12th Air Force moved Allied troops up the Italian boot through 1944 and finally pushed the Germans out.

The Mediterranean turned out to be anything but the "soft underbelly" Winston Churchill had promised. From the blowing sand of North Africa to the frigid winter of Germany, soldiers and airmen did what was asked of them, often at great cost but never without skill and determination.

THAR SHE BLOWS! Mount Vesuvius erupts in March 1944, right in the middle of a war. Lava cinders and debris covered a wide area of land in the vicinity of Naples. American serviceman Bill Skinner snapped this photo.

WACS ON PARADE. In Morocco, these women (above) marched with a national honor guard. Though women soldiers were not to participate in direct combat, many gave their lives for their country.

PUP ON WHEELS. Bill Skinner took this photo of armament officer Captain Kruzan on a motorcycle with his dog in Italy in 1943. After expelling the Germans, servicemen found all kinds of things from discarded jeeps to motorcycles to keep them entertained.

National Archives

Charles Jaslow

DESERT DINING. This chow line formed in the western desert of North Africa, 1943.

PACKED AND READY. Lieutenant Boon Haddock checks over his parachute at La Senia Airdrome, North Africa, April 1943. The P-38 pilot's 37th Fighter Squadron was working its way across the desert, slowly pushing the Germans out until they surrendered the next month and left Tunisia.

AFRICAN PATROL BASE. A Navy PBY Catalina flying boat (below) sits on the ramp at Port Lyautey, Morocco in front of the French administration building and the control tower. These bombers hunted for German U-boats out of this base, patrolling both the Atlantic and the Mediterranean Sea.

National Archives

James Stitt

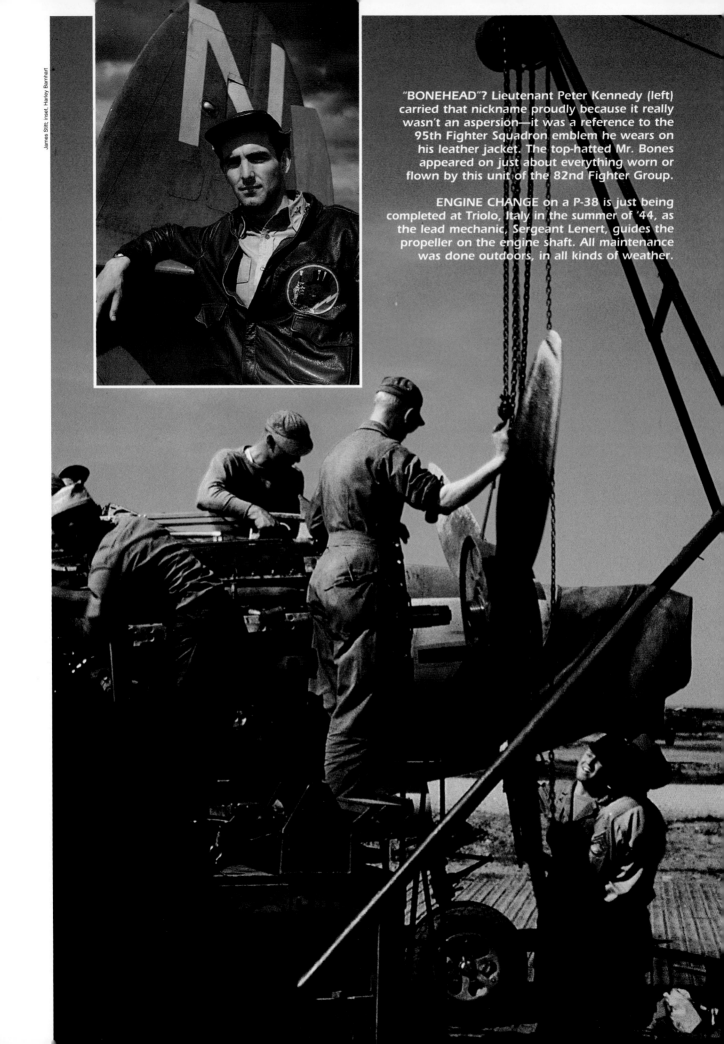

"BONEHEAD"? Lieutenant Peter Kennedy (left) carried that nickname proudly because it really wasn't an aspersion—it was a reference to the 95th Fighter Squadron emblem he wears on his leather jacket. The top-hatted Mr. Bones appeared on just about everything worn or flown by this unit of the 82nd Fighter Group.

ENGINE CHANGE on a P-38 is just being completed at Triolo, Italy in the summer of '44, as the lead mechanic, Sergeant Lenert, guides the propeller on the engine shaft. All maintenance was done outdoors, in all kinds of weather.

LUXURY STAFF QUARTERS. The 14th Fighter Group stayed here in the winter of 1944-45 at Triolo, Italy. The building was made of shipping crates, and heat was provided by high-octane aviation fuel from "drop tank" at right.

Photos: James Stitt

LOT'S ~ ROOM
PARACHUTE ~ SHOP

THRU THESE PORTALS PASS
THE WORLDS GREATEST
FIGHTER PILOTS

OPERATIONS

THE GREATEST FIGHTER PILOTS walked through these 37th Fighter Squadron operations building doors, and Lieutenant Mapes seems to agree with the assessment. Almost every fighter unit around the world, on land and sea, carried the same sign. A fighter pilot had to think he was the best or he wouldn't have the confidence needed to go up against a capable enemy.

CREW CHIEF AT WORK as the sun goes down at Triolo, Italy. The 37th Squadron P-38 below has been back from a mission for some time, and though the pilot is done, the ground crew has just started. They will work well into the night getting the fighter ready for the next day, rearming the machine guns and cannon ...hanging and refueling new drop tanks...checking engines.

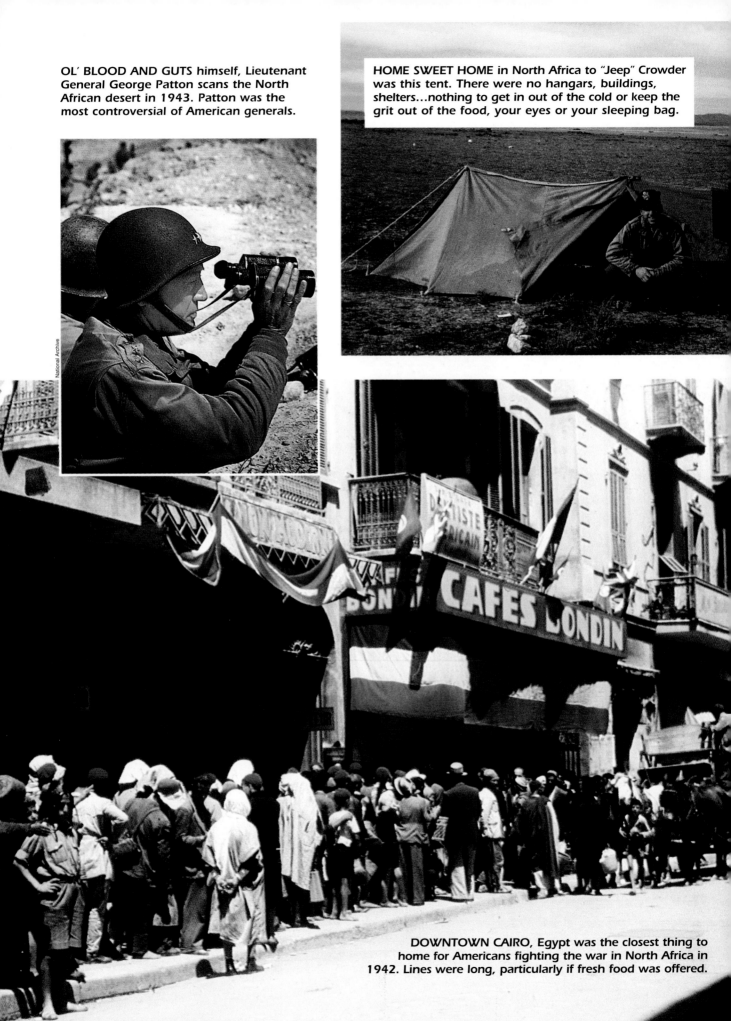

OL' BLOOD AND GUTS himself, Lieutenant General George Patton scans the North African desert in 1943. Patton was the most controversial of American generals.

HOME SWEET HOME in North Africa to "Jeep" Crowder was this tent. There were no hangars, buildings, shelters...nothing to get in out of the cold or keep the grit out of the food, your eyes or your sleeping bag.

DOWNTOWN CAIRO, Egypt was the closest thing to home for Americans fighting the war in North Africa in 1942. Lines were long, particularly if fresh food was offered.

NAPLES NEWS came in the form of "Yank" magazine, sold on the streets by Italians lucky enough to land the job. Flight surgeon Captain Bill "Doc" Curtis (left) of the 37th Fighter Squadron was happy to find anything to read in English besides military tech manuals. The war was cruel to Italy, which never had much taste for it anyway. When Mussolini was overthrown, the nation surrendered in September 1943 and immediately joined the Allied side.

OH-7 was the wish of every crapshooter in the service. This 321st Bomb Group B-25 crew in Algeria wants that kind of luck to rub off on their aircraft as they head out for a mission. Nose art became a phenomenon in World War II, appearing on everything from jeeps and tanks to bombers.

DOING THE LAUNDRY at the 320th Bomb Group's home field on Sardinia, 1944. In almost all combat zones, getting clothes clean was not only a mundane chore, it could be a nightmare. Some crews in the field used gasoline as a last resort, but this was hard on both the fibers and the skin...and you dare not smoke.

CHOW ON CORSICA in 1945 wasn't the greatest, but a table sure beat sitting on the ground. Flight chiefs Marlin Richardson (below left) and Willie Sheehan (center) seem to be digging in. Getting decent food in all theaters of war was difficult. Canned C rations and other packaged food was the order of the day, like it or not.

TWIN TROUBLE for the enemy were major Hugh "Rowdy" Dow and second lieutenant Glenn Dow (right). The twin brothers flew P-47 Thunderbolts with the 350th Fighter Group out of Italy at the end of the war. The War Department normally didn't permit such pairings after the loss of all five Sullivan brothers on a single ship at sea, but this time it made an exception.

LITTLE BIT OF HOME. Red Cross volunteers reached out across a war-torn world to help wherever possible. Clubs like this one in Italy (above) were havens of refuge and a small piece of home, particularly when staffed by good old-fashioned American girls. Just to hear a soft voice when the going was particularly rough did wonders.

YANKEE PILOT, BRITISH MACHINE. Army Air Forces Spitfire pilots were a unique breed...Americans flying British airplanes on reverse lend-lease. Jerry Carver (right) was attached to the 308th Fighter Squadron, 31st Fighter Group at Pomigliano, Italy in 1944 and he often flew fellow pilot Bill Skinner's Spitfire VIII, Lonesome Polecat, on fighter sweeps over the front lines.

JIMMY DOOLITTLE (left) was commanding general of the 12th Air Force in North Africa when he flew this American fighter group Spitfire in early 1943. Doolittle was one of the legendary fliers of all time, famous for racing unstable planes called Gee-Bees and for his research in instrument flying. In April 1942, he led a formation of B-25s off the deck of the aircraft carrier Hornet to bomb Tokyo and the surrounding area. He went on to command the 8th Air Force during the final year of the assault on Germany.

BASE ON THE BOOT. Italy became one massive air base for the American Air Force. Flying up the boot and into Germany, AAF planes hit everything from trucks to oil refineries...nothing moved without being in danger of getting bombed or strafed.

RED CROSS GIRLS—always cheerful and ready with a kind word— seemed to be in every theater, even under intense combat conditions, to hand out doughnuts and coffee. These 31st Fighter Group personnel at Castel Volturno, Italy didn't mind standing in line when they knew "their gal" was at the other end.

LIGHTNING STRIKES. Lieutenant Del Ryland smiles from the cockpit of his P-38 Lightning fighter in Foggia, Italy in 1945. Lightning pilots loved their aircraft, ideal for the Mediterranean theater with twin-engine safety for long over-water flights. Nothing settled a bomber crew's nerves like an escort of P-38s.

CANNES ON LEAVE. In 1945, the hotel shoreline at this French resort city was a soldier's dream with just about every form of relaxation available. Forgetting the war, for even short periods, was an important part of keeping combat personnel mentally healthy. What better place to do that than Cannes? (Although once the Mediterranean was free of the Germans, anywhere was wonderful if away from the fighting.)

A PIPER CUB ON FLOATS was perfect for survival training on the Italian coast, for taking men out to sea, then retrieving them. Training? Looks like too much fun to be called that, but what did it matter? Anything but being shot at was worthwhile.

National Archives

Robert Frizzell/Kenneth Kailey

GIRL FROM ROME. The Italian people were warm, friendly and very glad to see the Americans push the Germans out. Homes were opened in spite of grinding poverty, and battle-weary soldiers were offered hospitality at every turn. A friendly face like this girl's at left was balm to the soul.

SWEET TREAT IN THE HEAT. Some watermelon on the Mediterranean, near Tripolitania, is enjoyed by American servicemen Red Pittard and "Lydia" Pinkham (right) in the summer of 1943. The jeep provided a perfect serving table and the swimming was near perfect. It was times like this that made the war drift away, but not for long.

FOREIGN TROOPS of every nation took up arms during the war, though they were often hard to identify... the photographer who took this shot wasn't able to figure out who these soldiers were as they kept marching right on by.

Claude Porter

National Archives

DITCHING PRACTICE for this B-24 crew may have been fun but it was no game. The Liberator bomber was notorious for coming apart when it hit water. Left to right above are bombardier Charlie Masteller, co-pilot Gene Sebring, armorer Van Sickle and engineer Al Braddach.

STREET URCHIN. Boys like this one at Tarquinia (right) were a bitter fruit of war in Italy. American soldiers thought they had it rough until they looked into the eyes of these children.

DOPEY was drawn on the rudder of this P-40F by Lieutenant Charles "Jazz" Jaslow (below) with crayons, the only medium that he could find.

Robert Frizzell

LIGHTNING IN THE MUD at the 14th Fighter Group base near Triolo, Italy in late 1944. Mud was a constant in all theaters of operations. Pierced Steel Plank (PSP) was laid down, and it did keep the planes from getting stuck. But the mud oozed up through the holes, making the steel as slick as grease. When it wasn't muddy, it was so dusty the sand would get in everything, including fine-tuned engines. Who said this was going to be easy?

James Still

PEACEFUL HARBOR. Combat often glared in contrast to the calm surroundings in which it took place, like this tranquil European port.

CHAPTER FOUR

MEMORIES FROM EUROPE

The German Blitzkrieg conquered most of Europe by May 1940. From that time until the D-Day invasion of 1944, the war against Germany was waged at sea and from the air.

When the European war broke out in September 1939, the United States remained strongly isolationist. Nevertheless, an increasing number of American men joined the Royal Air Force, most through Canada. Hitler's invasion of Russia in June would prove to be his ultimate downfall.

With the U.S. entry into the war, the 8th Air Force was created in 1942 to initiate the only American combat operations from England. The "Mighty 8th", which grew to be a formidable force, started with a small nucleus of B-17 bombers.

After nearly being wiped out in 1943, American bombers were able to carry on, thanks to long-range escort fighters which flew along to protect them from enemy attack.

The Allies' Skies

In February and March 1944, American and German fighter pilots slugged it out as never before in the European skies, and the air war turned firmly in the Allies' favor.

By mid 1944, nothing was safe on the Continent as Allied fighters and medium bombers went after heavily defended airfields, trains, trucks, motorcycles …anything that moved.

While the P-51 Mustang reigned supreme in the high-altitude battles waged over Germany, the rugged P-47 Thunderbolt and sleek P-38 Lightning became the most effective ground-attack fighters of the war.

At last, on June 6, 1944, as the Soviet Union pitted its 400 divisions against Germany's 160 divisions on the eastern front, America, Britain, Canada and France opened the ground war on the western front.

Europe was invaded by 155,000 men in the largest force ever assembled. The east/west pincer sounded the death knell for the Third Reich, though the German Army was far from defeated.

What Sights to See

When they could take a break from the action, American boys fresh off the farm found Europe a fascinating blend of the ancient (anything over 150 years old was ancient to an American) and the exotic.

England represented a calm oasis in the storm, full of friendly kids and plenty of young girls ready to go out on the town.

Once in France on their way to Germany, soldiers watched 1,000-year-old towns blown to rubble with homeless children in the streets. Still, a stick of gum and a smile did wonders.

Liberated Paris was a dream, undamaged and wide open, with wonderful food and drink at streetside cafes. But however enjoyable, any rest and relaxation was short-lived.

By December 1944, the Germans counterattacked the Allies in what became known as the Battle of the Bulge. They temporarily stopped the Allied race across Europe for Germany.

By early 1945, Montgomery and Patton renewed their heated rivalry, trying to beat each other to Germany, often leaving their supply lines far behind.

The final months of the war in Europe were the scene of overwhelming Allied might as planes, tanks and soldiers poured into Germany from both sides.

This extraordinary witness of Allied strength and American industrial power was immediately turned into the rebuilding of rubble-strewn Europe under the Marshall Plan—a vast improvement from the post-World War I attitudes that planted the bitter seeds of World War II.

SWEET TREAT. GIs enjoy some ice cream along with a view of the Cathedral of Notre Dame in late summer 1944. The liberation of Paris happened on August 25, 1944.

GLACES

Choco

GLACES

CHOW TIME! These GIs in Germany line up for whatever the cook is going to give them. What's for dinner? That question didn't matter, as there were no choices and everything ran together in your cold mess kit anyway. Chow drew more complaints than most things during wartime, but the truth of the matter was American fighting men ate better than their enemies, who didn't enjoy the near-limitless supplies sent by motivated American workers back home.

MOVING ON. Refugees carry what's left of their belongings through the rubble of war-torn Europe. Families on the Continent paid a terrible price during World War II. Even though the Allies destroyed entire towns while moving through France and Belgium, these soldiers were welcomed with open arms as liberators. The American GI quickly became the friend of every kid he saw by giving away chewing gum and Hershey bars.

Photos: National Archives

BATTLE OF THE BULGE. M4 Sherman tanks of the 40th Tank Battalion sit in the snow awaiting the word to move forward at St. Vith, Belgium, December 1944, during one of the most famous of all World War II battles. The surprise German counterattack just before Christmas caught the Americans before anything could be done...the resulting western bulge in the front lines created the famous nickname. Brigadier General Anthony McAuliffe's 101st Airborne Division was trapped at Bastogne, a critical Belgian crossroads town, with no way out. When the Germans demanded surrender, McAuliffe's famous one word reply, "Nuts!", became legend.

National Archives

CLIP CLOP! You can almost hear the sound of this horse and wagon making its way along Oxford Street in London on a cold wet day in January 1945. An acute shortage of "petrol", as the British called gasoline, made for an odd mixture of horse-drawn carriages, coal-fueled trucks, taxis and military vehicles on the streets. If there was a constant in England, it was rain, but that didn't matter to American fighting men. Leave in London was a coveted gift, even when it was foggy and wet...there were shows, pubs, the Red Cross, USO clubs and maybe a date.

Byron Trent

PICCADILLY CIRCUS (above) remained the bustling center of London throughout the war, regardless of continual attack from German bombers and the infamous V-1 buzz bomb and V-2 ballistic missile. Double-deck buses, motorcars using the "wrong lanes" and breakneck traffic around this and other circular intersections in London left no doubt in an American's mind that he was, like the World War I song said, "over there".

BOMBER PILOTS of the 322nd Bomb Group at Great Saling, England, September 1943. From left, Captains Louis Sebille, Roland Scott and Howard Posson were among the first pilots to fly combat in the B-26 Marauder from England.

A LITTLE "R AND R". Red Cross girls and soldiers of the 34th Division enjoy the sun deck at the 5th Army rest center near Rome, June 1944. The former Mussolini Youth Center had room for 2,500 soldiers, so it was always bustling with much-needed activity and laughter for troops just off the front lines.

"TAXI!" In London, a sailor waits to board the favored mode of city transportation in front of an air raid shelter. London cabbies were some of the most respected men in England.

FIRE FIGHTERS. Private Stephen and Corporal Venarchik kept vigil over the B-17 Flying Fortresses at their 91st Bomb Group base of Bassingbourn, England. Despite being ribbed for living in the relative luxury of England, Army bomber crews had the highest casualty rate of the war. When battle-damaged Forts limped back to base, often on fire, they needed rapid response from crash crews.

REAL HORSEPOWER. A horse-drawn ale wagon sits on a London side street in 1944. Unchanged for centuries, English beer wagons like this one remained useful during the war since they used no fuel vital to the war effort. The sturdy team of workhorses above likely did well enough on hay or oats.

CAFE IN PARIS. The GIs at right enjoy the civilized pleasure of the Cafe George V on a wonderful September 1944 afternoon in Paris. The American, British and French flags above the awning say everything about how the French felt...liberation was sweet.

BOGGED DOWN. The infantry battalion jeep below is stuck in the mud of what used to be a beautiful Cologne street. Among those trying to wrestle it out is a German civilian. Such a contrast was becoming normal by early 1945, as the German populace came to depend on the new conquerors for sustenance. Just beyond this point, both sides were shelling each other across the Rhine River, the rounds whistling overhead the minor drama of a stuck jeep.

John Quincy/Stanley Wyglendowski

CLOSE SHAVE. Supply Section Sergeant Melvin Crooks is shaving, 9th Air Force style, above. If Sergeant Crooks had some hot water in the field, he was lucky...but the heat likely didn't last very long in his "tin pot" helmet. This scene was photographed at one of the 9th's first forward airfields on the Continent, established just after D-Day. Tour-en-Bessim, France was ahead of the Normandy beachhead at the base of the Cherbourg peninsula as the 9th kept up with the 1st and 3rd Armies in July 1944.

Stanley Wyglendowski

OLDE ENGLAND. Main Street of Bishop's Stortford, Essex was a glimpse into early England for young Americans from a country not even 200 years old. The bicycle was the primary means of wartime personal transportation.

John Quincy/Stanley Wyglendowski

National Archives

P-47 CREW CHIEF Sergeant P.W. Mutting sits in the cockpit of his fighter (all planes were considered to be "on loan" to the pilot) during a major inspection at Asch, Belgium, spring 1945. The Thunderbolt was the finest ground-attack fighter of the war, with its rugged construction, eight .50-caliber machine guns and the ability to carry bombs.

A SCOTTISH LASS gets some warm attention from her two countrymen. Scotland's troops fought across the globe in World War II.

GAME OF DARTS passes the time in England as soldiers below anticipate the invasion of Normandy, late spring 1944. The smiles hide the very real tension about the unknown as these men wait for word that D-Day was on. When the invasion was finally launched on June 6, 1944, 4,000 men died in the toughest fighting of the war.

DODGE AMBULANCE (left) crosses the 210-foot-long makeshift bridge over the Serchio River, Italy. The original bridge, seen in the background, was destroyed, so U.S. Army engineers simply replaced it in short order. Often unheralded, these battlefield miracle workers were crucial to moving Allied troops and equipment forward, often under fire.

MP CHECKPOINT. Sergeant Andrew Para (above) checks the credentials of a Belgian farmer near the canal running through Namur, Belgium.

MISSION BRIEFING for fighter pilots of the 355th Fighter Squadron (below) at Ober-Olm, Germany during the last month of the war. By that time, Allied pilots were flying off German soil against German targets.

LIBERATION OF PARIS becomes reality as American and French troops roll through the Arc de Triomphe on August 25, 1944. Troops of the U.S. 3rd Army crossed the Seine River that morning, and General Dwight Eisenhower ordered the French 2nd Armored Division to lead the way into the French capital.

AMERICAN SONGS were longed for by GIs overseas. Red Cross girl above enjoys some hometown music with boys from the 34th Division at the 5th Army rest center, Italy, June 1944.

HOME AWAY FROM HOME. The ever-present Army pyramidal tent became a fixture around the world. The one at right was pitched at Criqueville, just off the Normandy beachhead, in June 1944.

RAPT ATTENTION is a requirement for the P-47 pilots of the 56th Fighter Group below during a January 1944 mission briefing at Halesworth, England. Among this group of men are several aces, those with five or more enemy aircraft destroyed—including 27-victory ace Bob Johnson, third from the left, fourth row. These men knew how to use the large Thunderbolt, clearly evident since the 56th finished the war with over 1,000 kills.

Air Force Museum

MISSION AHEAD. Captain Dick Perley leaves the operations tent at Toul-Ochey, near Nancy, France, and heads to his P-47 for a mission. He holds his kneeboard with mission briefing card in his right hand.

ENLISTED MEN'S TENT AREA housed the 320th Bomb Group at Longecourt, France, early 1945. Anyone lucky enough to have a stove had to keep it burning all the time.

Joseph Kingsbury

ENGLISH BAILEY BRIDGE serves these Americans crossing the river near Ponetta in the high Italian mountains, December 20, 1944. The area was occupied by U.S. and Brazilian troops as a funnel point for chasing the Germans north, and the renowned Bailey design was crucial to making it happen. A small team of engineers could lay out and erect a Bailey in a relatively short period of time, providing the Allies with the ability to ignore downed bridges as they pushed their way through Europe.

NORMANDY RUINS. A nun and two French children look through all that's left of St. Molo Catholic Church, Valognes, just north of St. Mere Eglise on the Cherbourg peninsula. In spite of losing so much, the French remained grateful for regaining their freedom.

MAIL FROM HOME was one of the strongest morale boosters for anyone overseas. The men on this rocket launcher-equipped Sherman tank seem to be totally absorbed by this brief respite from the war, even if the mail was shared.

WAITING FOR A LIFT. Officers and enlisted men look for a truck to take them to town from England's Wormingford airfield in the early evening of August 30, 1944. English hospitality was shown to most GIs.

Opposite and above: National Archives

National Archives

Edward Richie

ALLIED IN SONG. Russians and Americans meet on the Rhine River for the first time (above) in March 1945. Some German accordions were found in Torgau by the Russians and were used to celebrate the meeting of the U.S. 69th Infantry Division, 1st Army and the 58th Russian Guards Division, 1st Ukrainian Army.

Glenn Tessmer

SURPLUS PLANE PARTS were used to build the runabout above at the 4th Fighter Group's base, Debden, England. The fenders are fuel "drop tanks", while the sheet metal and plexiglass windows came from wrecked aircraft on the field.

CO-PILOT'S VIEW. Photo at right, shot from a B-24 of the 329th Squadron, 93rd Bomb Group, shows tell-tale trails of sky markers from the preceding formations. The smoke markers were used to identify the target for lead pilots and bombardiers. The other aircraft in the formation usually dropped their bombs when the lead ship let go. This mission happened on December 24, 1944.

BRIDGE ACROSS THE RHINE. Army trucks cross the Alexander Patch heavy pontoon bridge across the Rhine on March 28, 1945. Built by the 85th Engineers, the bridge became a key thoroughfare for moving Allied troops forward in the last weeks of the war. The bridges at Remagen and other Rhine River locations were the focal points of fierce fighting since both sides realized their strategic importance.

BRITISH BICYCLE BOY. Child below looks down a back street in a small Suffolk village near an American bomber base. The friendly American "invasion" had a strong influence on English children, who got chewing gum ("Any gum, chum?" they'd ask) and other things from their new friends. Despite strict security regulations, children were given the run of all American airfields to pal around with the crews and crawl through the airplanes.

PRACTICE BOMBS are prepared for loading into a 466th Bomb Group B-24 Liberator at Attlebridge, England, 1944. In spite of wartime pressures to mount continual raids into enemy territory, practice bombing was crucial to introducing new crews to combat procedures and to keeping operational groups highly trained.

LOADING UP. An anti-aircraft gun loader drops a clip of shells into the breech on a hot summer day in Europe (below). A ring of these guns surrounded most American installations and lined the gunnels of ships, creating a formidable defense against enemy aircraft.

USAF

D-PLUS 5, SOUTHERN FRANCE. Five days after the Allied invasion of southern France, the beach west of St. Rafael was crammed with landing craft.

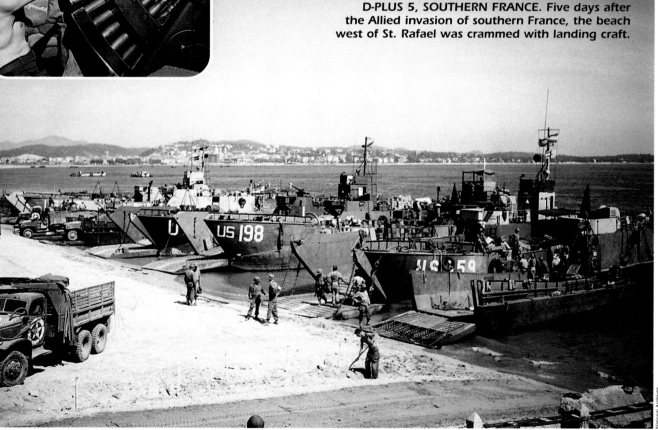

National Archives

FIGHTING MAN'S BEST FRIEND. A land-locked sailor crouches down with his dog in a Navy salvage depot at Anzio (right). The warmth and affection of a pet was amplified in combat, where so few things were humanizing. Dogs seemed to show up everywhere, even at 30,000 feet flying in bombers, with their own jury-rigged oxygen masks.

A RUGGED LIFESAVER. This American ambulance traveling through the English countryside was a dependable workhorse. A basic Dodge truck chassis beneath its shell was versatile and simple, giving Army mechanics commonality between many different vehicles, particularly important in the field.

GIs IN PARIS enjoy some time off at a cafe where the owners have made sure their loyalties are displayed very clearly. The words are obvious enough, but also included on the panels below the windows are the national markings applied to British, Free French and American aircraft. This was about as close to the "life of Riley" as anyone got in war-torn Europe.

DOWN BY THE RIVERSIDE. Cambridge, England was a hub of activity for American servicemen based throughout the East Anglian countryside. The Cam River was a relaxing and entertaining place, and its banks always seemed to have dozens of pretty English girls to pass the time with. This didn't sit too well with jealous Englishmen, but that didn't seem to stop anyone.

Edward Richie

Mark Brown/USAFA

BRITAIN'S FIRST JET AIRCRAFT, the Gloster E.28/39, sits on display (above) in wartime London with a biplane Walrus amphibian, a fabric-covered anachronism at the dawn of the jet age. The tiny Gloster flew for the first time on May 15, 1941, 2 years after the Germans flew their first jet and a year and a half before the Americans got the twin-engine XP-59 off the Muroc dry lake bed that would eventually become Edwards Air Force Base. The first jets had no more performance than propeller-driven types, but it was a beginning.

AIRCRAFT NOSE ART became a phenomenon in World War II as crews decorated bombers and fighters with personal nicknames and art. "Ruby's Raiders" carried the likeness of the WAC voted most beautiful in wartime England, while "5 Grand" was the 5,000th B-17 Flying Fortress built by Boeing in Seattle...everyone who worked on it signed it. Following the tradition of knights who carried decorated shields, combat airmen took comfort and confidence in facing death with the luck given by their own personal aircraft.

Mark Brown/USAFA

THREE GIs IN A PUNT head down the Cam River in Cambridge, England during some much-needed time off.

GERMAN PRISONERS OF WAR line up for classification at Bolzano, Italy, May 1945. When the war ended on May 8, the Allies found themselves with hundreds of thousands of prisoners to repatriate.

ONE HORSEPOWER. Fun on England's southeast coast took many forms, but this ingenious "Victory Bomber", seen by serviceman Edward Richie on a Channel beach, was truly unique.

DOUBLE DATE. American Army officers on leave take out two English girls. A date was the single most sought after event by a serviceman overseas. As a result, hundreds of men brought home English war brides in spite of tight controls and years of paperwork.

National Archives

National Archives

MEETING AT THE RHINE. At Torgau, Germany, U.S. Army Major General E.F. Reinhard, Commander, 69th Infantry Division, 1st Army, greets Major General Rusakov, 58th Russian Guards Division, 1st Ukrainian Army, March 1945. This longed-for event signaled the end of the Third Reich...the two largest armies in the world had been pushing toward Germany from both sides and had finally joined at this small town. The Russians had paid a terrible price for victory... upwards of 26 million killed. Their ability to absorb and occupy vast portions of the German Army was pivotal in winning the war, giving the Allies on other fronts much smaller forces to fight

NAZI "ARCHITECTURE".
German pillbox above is effectively hidden with a camouflage paint job in 1944. At a casual glance, this bunker looks as if it's one of the houses on a quiet street in France. The result could be deadly, unless Allied intelligence was able to spot the fakes on reconnaissance photos taken before troops moved forward.

A BANG-UP FOURTH.
Sergeants Bob Sand and Russell Butts obviously decided some Fourth of July fireworks were in order back in 1944. Bob, on right, pretends to light the fuse on a 500-pound bomb while Russell plugs his ears in expectation. Jokes like this helped make day-to-day life in Army units a bit less monotonous.

CHAPTER FIVE

THE BIG NAMES

From world leaders to the military brass to beloved entertainers of the day, who can forget the legendary names from the Victory Era?

The 20th century's leaps in communications and transportation technology allowed World War II to be run directly by the leaders of each nation.

Though the Tripartite Axis of Germany-Italy-Japan was supposed to be a cooperative effort, Hitler did what he wanted without much advice, as did Tojo. The Allied effort worked far differently.

America, Great Britain and Russia were coordinated by major meetings and continual communication between Roosevelt, Churchill and Stalin. When they couldn't meet face-to-face, they sent personal representatives. Despite many differences, they saw their common enemy with striking clarity.

Franklin Roosevelt was a hands-on president who didn't let polio stop him for a minute. Though he remains controversial for some of his far-reaching social programs and running for four terms, he was tireless in his prosecution of the war, an ideal leader for such a time.

Nation Mourned Fatherly Figure

His smiling face and ringing words brought strength on the home front and in the theaters of war. When he died, less than a month before V-E Day, the nation mourned his death as if a family member had passed.

Winston Churchill and Joseph Stalin were equally strong leaders who lived in their war rooms below the streets of London and Moscow, getting very little sleep.

Few orators were ever the equal of Churchill. His ringing words of courage and determination, from his election as Prime Minister in May 1940 to the end of the war, symbolized the sheer tenacity of the British fighting spirit.

Though wary of Stalin and the rise of communism in Europe, Churchill could get along with him on equal terms. Each respected the other, if often doubting the truth of what they heard. Stalin, who was direct commander in chief of his forces in even the small decisions, was able to defeat the German Army at his very gates.

When war broke out, every American citizen was called on to do his or her part. Nowhere was the response more visible than in the entertainment industry.

Performers Helped the Cause

Actors and actresses, singers, musicians, dancers, vaudevillians, radio personalities…all came forward by the hundreds to sell war bonds and make extensive overseas USO tours for the troops.

Bob Hope was the master…he seemed to be in every theater of war at the same time, bright and cheerful, full of energy. He hid the exhaustion and lack of sleep well, since he wanted to give the men and women so far from home a ray of hope, a taste of home, before they went off to battle.

Some famous entertainers, including Carole Lombard, lost their lives while working without pay on behalf of Uncle Sam, while others enlisted in the armed forces directly and either served Stateside or went off to combat.

Wayne Morris and Robert Taylor became naval aviators, Jimmy Stewart flew B-24 bombers in combat, Clark Gable flew several combat missions as a B-17 gunner, and Ronald Reagan, William Holden, Craig Stevens, William Wyler, Lloyd Bridges, Lee J. Cobb and many others made training films with the Army Air Forces' first motion picture unit.

ROBERT TAYLOR became a naval aviator during the war. As a lieutenant in the U.S. Navy Reserve, the actor applied for combat duty but was repeatedly turned down and assigned as an instructor teaching fledgling pilots how to fly. The Navy used him extensively in making training films.

BOB HOPE introduces dancer Patty Thomas at a fighter base in England in 1944, during one of Bob's numerous overseas USO jaunts. Hope and his band seemed to be everywhere at once, doing more for morale than an army of entertainers.

"FRANCES LANGFORD, WORTH FIGHTING FOR" was Bob Hope's usual sly introduction when the two of them took the stage. The GIs crammed around this stage at Palermo, Sicily in 1943 didn't seem to notice the close quarters as long as Bob, Frances, Jerry Colonna, Tony Romano and the rest of the troupe were in action.

National Archives

National Archives

GENE KELLY, like so many others in Hollywood, answered the call to wartime service and joined the Navy. Often, instead of getting to do his job, he was called out for public relations or recruiting.

LORD LOUIS MOUNTBATTEN (above left), Supreme Commander, Southeast Asia Command, and commando operations master, confers with Army pilots Colonel Phil Cochran and Major R.T. Smith (right) during the planning for a combined air-ground commando raid into Burma.

PRESIDENT ROOSEVELT meets Saudi Arabia's King Ibn Saud on the USS Quincy in Cairo, with Admiral William D. Leahy (left) looking on, in February 1945.

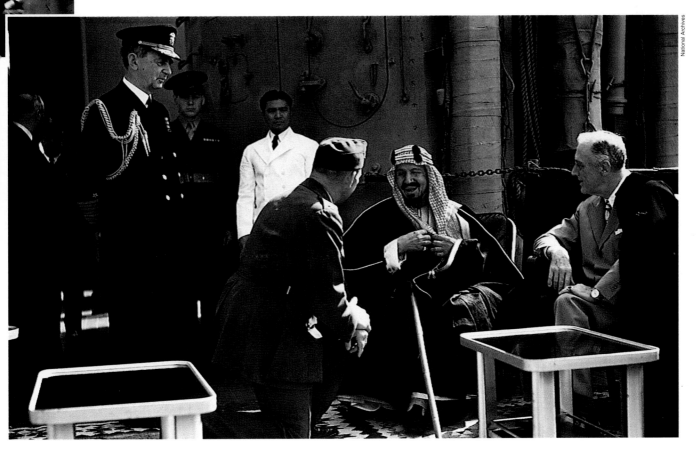

National Archives

KING GEORGE VI, Lieutenant General Mark Clark (Commander, U.S. 5th Army) and General Sir Harold Alexander salute the troops in Italy on January 2, 1944. England's King was visiting the two top Allied command leaders in the theater.

National Archives

EDDIE "ROCHESTER" ANDERSON, the gravel-voiced foil on Jack Benny's radio program, made several overseas USO tours, including one to England (below).

Edward Richie

National Archives

EDWARD "BUTCH" O'HARE became one of the Navy's first war heroes. He earned the Medal of Honor by shooting down several Japanese planes attacking his aircraft carrier. Chicago's major airport was named after him.

EATIN' CHIEFS. The American Joint Chiefs of Staff take a meal together during the war. From left to right are Army Air Forces General H.H. "Hap" Arnold, Navy Admirals William D. Leahy and Ernest J. King and Army General George C. Marshall. These four men determined the course of the war from the American side.

THE BIG THREE, Winston Churchill, Franklin D. Roosevelt and Joseph Stalin, meet in Yalta in February of 1945 to plan the forthcoming invasion of Europe. Behind them are some of their top military leaders.

ROOSEVELT AND CHURCHILL meet at Cairo, November 1943. Along with China's Chiang Kai-shek, they made final plans for the Pacific war and stated, "Japan shall be stripped of all islands in the Pacific which she has seized or occupied" since World War I along with all occupied Chinese territory. For the first time the Allies agreed that unconditional surrender would be demanded.

REICHSMARSCHALL HERMANN GOERING sits dejectedly in defeat just after being taken into custody by U.S. soldiers, May 1945. Germany's number-two man under Hitler, the former World War I fighter ace had built the Luftwaffe into the strongest air force in the world by the late 1930s. Goering's monumental mismanagement and lavish life-style eventually doomed German airpower. Sentenced to death in October 1946 at the Nuremberg war crimes trials, he swallowed cyanide before he could be hanged.

USAF

National Archives

Dennis Glen Cooper

National Archives

HENRY FONDA became a naval officer and, after much persuasion, got himself assigned to combat duty at sea, where he served with distinction.

GARY COOPER was photographed (right) at Hollandia during a 1944 USO tour of New Guinea. Actress Una Merkel (right) accompanied him on the tour.

GENERAL Dwight Eisenhower stands next to RAF Air Chief Marshall Arthur Tedder (right) on May 7, 1945, after giving a speech on the Allied victory over Germany. He is still holding the pen used to sign the surrender document.

GENERAL DOUGLAS MACARTHUR reads the Japanese surrender proclamation on the battleship Missouri, September 2, 1945, in front of (from left) Lieutenant General Kuzma Derevyanko (USSR), General Sir Thomas Blamey (Australia), Colonel Lawrence Moore-Cosgrave (Canada), General Jacques Le Clerc (France), Admiral Helfrich (Netherlands) and Air Vice Marshall L.M. Isitt (New Zealand).

National Archives

JAPAN'S DELEGATION on the USS Missouri included (foreground, from left) Minister Mamora Shigemitsu, signing for the emperor, and General Yoshijiro Umezu, signing for Imperial Japanese Army High Command.

National Archives

National Archives

PRESIDENT HARRY TRUMAN and Admiral Chester Nimitz at the White House during Nimitz Day in 1945. Nimitz led the U.S. Navy in the Pacific to victory.

CLAIRE LEE CHENNAULT (left) led his American Volunteer Group of pilots, the Flying Tigers, against the Japanese in China. Below, Tiger R.T. Smith poses in Kunming, China next to one of the group's famous P-40 fighters. No. 68 was usually flown by Charles "Chuck" Older, who later became famous as the judge in the Charles Manson trial. Both men became aces flying as hired guns for the Chinese.

R.T. Smith

CHAPTER SIX

THE NAVY ON LAND AND SEA

In December of 1941, the U.S. Navy had eight battleships, four aircraft carriers and one escort carrier. By September 1945, the service had grown to 5,788 warships and 66,000 landing vessels.

The Pacific war replaced the battleship with the aircraft carrier as the world's major military ship. Once ridiculed by the battleship admirals, U.S. naval aviation grew from an orphan service to the mightiest naval striking force in the world with 16 large aircraft carriers and 125 escort carriers with 400,000 personnel.

In combat, the U.S. Navy matched the ferocity and skill of Germany's U-boat crews and Japan's aircraft carrier pilots. The U.S. Navy's submarines proved devastating in the Pacific, as American sub commanders stalked and sank Japan's merchant fleet. Ship-based fighter planes, meanwhile, attacked nearly anything that sailed.

Although the U.S. lost 157 naval vessels (subs, frigates and larger ships) and 866 merchant ships (over 200 tons), Japan lost 433 and 2,346 respectively.

In one morning, the Pearl Harbor attack had increased Japan's imperial Asia/Pacific domain to 20 million square miles. Japanese victories came in heady gulps for the next 6 months...until the Battle of Midway, when American carrier planes put three of four enemy carriers out of action in just 5 minutes.

Navy Put Japan on the Run

From that point on, the U.S. Navy had Japan on the defensive, and the island nation quickly became overextended and undersupplied, unable to compete with American industrial might.

Japan depended on secure ocean routes for raw materials and enough food to keep its military in the field, but by the end of 1944, half its merchant fleet had been sunk, primarily by American submarines. By the end of the war, only 5% of that fleet existed.

With the U.S. Marine invasion of Guadalcanal in August 1942, Japanese forces began a bitter retreat marked by an increasing willingness to fight to the last man.

Heavy Tolls on Atolls

Soon tiny coral atolls with strange-sounding names became synonymous with terrible losses on both sides...Tarawa, Kwajelein, Saipan, Iwo Jima, Okinawa. At Iwo in February 1945, the Marines lost 6,821 men in 6 days to take 10 square miles. It was the costliest battle in the history of the Corps.

U.S. naval air forces were so effective they managed to neutralize the primary enemy naval and air bastion of Truk without an invasion.

At the end of 1944 came the Kamikaze aircraft suicide attacks, the enemy threat most dreaded by American sailors. With fanatical devotion, Japanese pilots inflicted the heaviest U.S. Navy losses of the war.

In the Battle of the Atlantic, the U.S. Navy supported the Royal Navy in mounting an increasingly effective anti-submarine campaign to stop the U-boat menace, and in launching the invasions of North Africa, Sicily and Normandy.

By the end of World War II, the U.S. fleet was larger than the combined strength of the world's navies at the beginning of the conflict. In spite of heavy American ship losses, industry resupplied them over and over again, something no nation on earth could match.

FIGHTERS OF THE USS YORKTOWN get ready to launch a strike against the Marshall and Gilbert Island chain during the November-December 1943 campaign.

National Archives

LANDING CRAFT BOARD their mother ship during practice for the 1944 D-Day invasion of Normandy. Such drills were often as dangerous as combat in the rough cold waters of the English Channel.

LOADING FOR D-DAY, an LST takes on as many trucks as it can carry before heading for the invasion of France.

National Archives

AERIAL GUNNER Airman Second Class Jack Cain earned three battle stars aboard the Avenger behind him. Sitting in the back of a slow, vulnerable torpedo bomber was more than a little dangerous.

A PBY CATALINA FLYING BOAT beached for servicing gets some needed attention. The "Cat" was really a 1930s design, but it showed up in combat until the end of the war, doing everything from long-range patrol to night torpedo attack.

WAITING FOR D-DAY in an English harbor, these landing craft are fueled and ready with a full complement of sailors and troops.

CONVOY PATROL. A Navy K-Type blimp covers cargo ships in the Atlantic Ocean (left). Not very well known, Navy blimps did outstanding anti-submarine hunting when the German U-boat menace was at its height, accounting for numerous sinkings.

SAIPAN SERVICE. Martin flying boat (below) is refueled off the coast of this island in April 1945. Navy seaplanes were used extensively in combat, particularly for night patrol bombing aided by radar (seen rising between the wings). Called "Mariners", these dependable planes sunk many thousands of tons of enemy shipping.

Photos: National Archives

THE DESTROYER USS BUCHANAN cruises alongside the aircraft carrier Wasp in June 1942. The destroyer is running "at speed", awaiting transfer of fuel or material. Destroyers were the roving protectors of Navy task forces.

THE INVASION OF MOROTAI as viewed from LCS-3, September 15, 1944. This massive landing craft could carry smaller troop landing craft, steaming up to the beach and letting them go, giving true close invasion support. Unlike so many other Pacific islands, Morotai fell with little resistance.

CARRIER LAUNCH! An Avenger torpedo bomber just off the deck of the carrier Yorktown, 1944, with the USS New Orleans ahead (above).

"SCRAPPY" gets some warm attention (above right) from Airman Third Class Robert L. Brown, Denver, Colorado. Pets, particularly dogs, were morale boosters.

LOADING TURRET GUNS of a PB4Y-1 Liberator was a long job for the armorer below. The patrol bomber was fitted with four power turrets and several swivel mounted guns.

"PLANE GUARDING" was a crucial task for small Navy cutters like this one covering the carrier Essex in the Gulf of Paria, Trinidad. If an airplane went into the sea, these vessels could be on the scene rapidly.

TIGHT SQUEEZE. The Panama Canal was an American war asset, enabling fleets to cross from one ocean to another quite quickly...but it sure could be a tight fit! Here, in 1943, the carrier Yorktown is barely squeezing through with inches to spare...great entertainment for both the sailors and those ashore.

CATAPULT CREW PORTSIDE works on a damaged catapult track. A carrier could operate in World War II without this powerful slingshot, but it meant the ship had to go quite a bit faster. The catapult officer, with "Fly 1" on his jersey, is talking with the "green crew". Everyone on a flight deck had color-coded shirts indicating their jobs to help eliminate some confusion during complex carrier operations.

ABANDON SHIP DRILL on the battleship Missouri (below) looks orderly, and most seem to have their life jackets on. Such drills were standard procedure since no one knew when it might happen for real. Fortunately, battleships were about the toughest ships in the fleet. The OS2U Kingfisher float plane (background) was used as a scout for the fleet and a rescue craft.

Photos: National Archives

AT MASSACRE BAY off Attu in the Aleutian Islands, three MTBs (motor torpedo or PT boats) and a PBY Catalina refuel from the USS Gillis on June 21, 1943. The Navy made sure refuelers like the Gillis were in place where and when needed.

TO THE POINT. Darts in the hangar room seem to be just what Seaman Second Class J.B. Chadwick needs at the naval air station in Norfolk, Virginia, April 20, 1945.

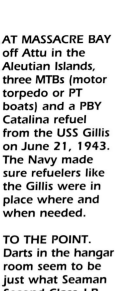

ESCORT CARRIER SANGAMON (below), with SBD Dauntlesses and F4F Wildcats, heads for Operation Torch, the invasion of North Africa in November 1942. The painted directions on the deck give heading and distances for pilots.

PT BOAT on a practice run (left) off New York on August 20, 1943. Though PT crews got much of the glamour as dashing sailors, they also took heavy losses. To deliver their torpedoes accurately, they had to get in close, putting them in range of enemy guns.

NAVY PILOT below has just returned from a mission in 1943. The "Mae West" life preserver and parachute saved many Navy fliers in trouble.

A JIVE BAND on the USS New Mexico (below) plays next to this battleship's 14-inch stern guns. In many ways, Navy ships provided the best variety of entertainment, food and living conditions— though those below decks would have loved air-conditioning. Army men and Marines often tried to get aboard a ship for a meal, particularly battleships and carriers with immense galleys.

STRIKING POWER. A U.S.
Navy battleship goes through a test firing sequence during her shakedown cruise, October 1943. The battleship forever lost its place to the carrier as America's primary ship during World War II. The struggle through the 1920s and '30s had been vicious between the "battleship admirals" and airpower advocates like the Army's Billy Mitchell and the Navy's William A. Moffett.

DEVASTATED FLEET. When American ships pulled into the harbor at Toulon after the invasion of southern France, U.S. sailors were greeted with the remnants of the once proud French fleet. When France fell to Germany, most of the fleet remained under the collaborating Vichy government. Targeted by Allies, the ships were destroyed and Toulon harbor was soon clogged with sunken hulks.

Photos: National Archives

DEBARKATION, JUNE 1944. Infantry men board landing craft that will take them to troop ships for D-Day. Southern English harbors were clogged just before the Normandy invasion and Allied planners were worried the concentration of men and equipment would be a juicy target. The barrage balloons next to the harbor terminal were run up every day, but the Luftwaffe never showed up, a massive miscalculation on Hitler's part.

"I'LL RAISE YOU!" Poker games like the one at left on the USS New Mexico were a steady diversion during the long months at sea.

WAVEOFF AT SUNSET. F6F Hellcat at right aborts its landing approach to the carrier Randolph, framed by the ship's 40mm anti-aircraft guns. Planes were brought aboard by a landing signal officer (LSO), who used a set of paddles to tell the pilot how to maneuver his aircraft to a "trap" or one of the cables strung across the deck. The LSO's word was law...if he waved you off, he had reason.

DAZZLING CAMOUFLAGE adorns the French cruiser SS Gloire. The idea was certainly clear...make the attacker think there were no straight lines on the object and spoil his aim. Unfortunately, ships like the Gloire were so large that camouflage distortions didn't help very much.

KING NEPTUNE PARTY (top and above) added a little
levity aboard the carrier Wasp, June 1942. The high jinks
aboard Navy ships crossing the equator had become
legend by World War II. Those "sprogs" who'd never
crossed were inducted into the fraternity by King Neptune,
his "queen" and their court. Anything went, from dunking
the captain of the ship in a vat of old cooking fat mixed
with sugar to "burying" officers on deck in elaborate
coffins. The fun of the event took pressure off life at sea.

AT THE CUT. A TBF Avenger receives the "cut
signal" (pull throttle to idle) from the LSO on the
USS Charger, April 22, 1944. Coming back aboard
a carrier was the most dangerous part of Navy flying.

KINGFISHER ON THE SLED. An OS2U pilot pulls up onto the rubber beaching sled being pulled by the USS Quincy. This was a very involved operation as the pilot had to power up onto the sled, hook on, then secure a hoist to be lifted up onto the ship.

TRANSPORT SHIP USS President Adams sits at anchor in New Caledonia, July 1942. These ships were the lifeblood of the Pacific War. The Japanese found this out when the U.S. sunk most of their transport ships.

OIL CHANGE. Mechanics at left drain the oil from an F6F Hellcat during periodic maintenance. The never-ending job of keeping carrier aircraft in fighting trim fell to these men who rarely got above deck.

NEXT STOP, NORMANDY. Medics and litter bearers board an LCT (right) in preparation for the D-Day landings in Normandy.

TORPEDO PLANES "run up" on the carrier Enterprise, May 29, 1944 (below). "The Big E" finished the war as the Navy's most decorated carrier, having fought from Pearl Harbor in 1941 to Okinawa in 1945. Her planes participated in sinking three of the four Japanese carriers in the Battle of Midway, the turning point of the Pacific War.

Photos: National Archives

"THE FIGHTING LADY". The carrier Yorktown (right) earned her nickname through 2 years of continual combat operations— she was the second of the massive Essex class carriers that dominated the Pacific. Able to strike at any target with near impunity, these ships displaced 27,500 tons and had flight decks stretching 886 feet 1 inch by 89 feet 10 inches. The below-deck hangars were so large pilots could start engines and warm up below, cutting launch time significantly. This photo was taken August 4, 1943, just before her first combat operations against Marcus Island.

A LITTLE SACK TIME is put to good use by the PBY Catalina pilot below at his base in New Guinea, March 1944.

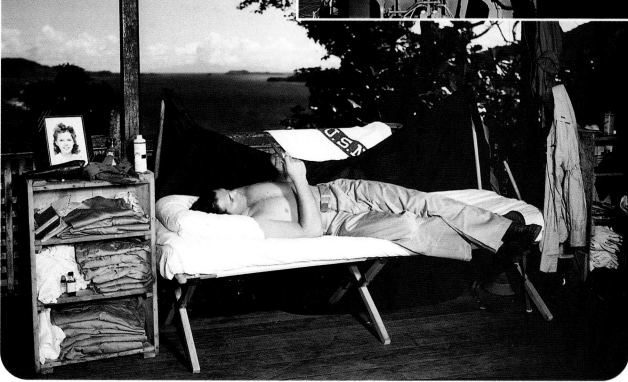

SOME UNSUNG HEROES

World War II broke the barriers to sex and race discrimination on an unprecedented scale. Women and black Americans, though often segregated into special units, were trained and integrated into both the military services and industry.

Women, in particular, entered by the hundreds of thousands, joining the WAVES, WACs, SPARS, Women Marines, WAFS and WASPs.

Government propagandists created "Rosie the Riveter" as the stalwart symbol of American womanhood gone to work until the men could return.

Earning Their Way

Some 3 million women went to work to aid the war effort, but millions more worked because they had to support families, as more than 1 million fathers were drafted and gone.

Many unions tried to keep women out or prevent them from getting equal pay, but the demands of war forced the issue. In addition, women took leadership in home-front activities like civil defense and growing victory gardens.

The Women's Army Corps (WAC) increased from one officer and 727 enlisted in July 1942 to 5,746 officers and 93,542 enlisted in April 1945. Some 10,000 went overseas and about 40,000 were assigned to the Air Force.

The Navy Women's Reserve (WAVES) had 86,000 on duty and another 11,000 in the Navy Nurse Corps. The most visible women in uniform were the Women's Auxiliary Ferrying Squadron (WAFS), then the 1,200 Women Airforce Service Pilots (WASPs), who flew the latest fighters and bombers in non-combat duty in order to free male pilots for fighting.

Never inducted into the Army Air Forces, they remained a part of the civil service and did not get veterans benefits until more than 30 years after the war. In all services, hundreds of women were killed in the line of duty or became POWs, often under fire.

Separate But Equal

The official "separate but equal" policy of the U.S. military kept black and white servicemen in segregated units.

The Army Air Forces established an all-black fighter squadron, which eventually turned into the 332nd Fighter Group serving in North Africa and Italy. The unit did extremely well, and by the end of the war became the only American fighter group never to lose a bomber under its escort protection.

By spring 1943, of 504,000 American troops overseas, 79,000 were black, most of them as non-combat service troops. Under pressure from Roosevelt, the Army set up two black divisions to enter combat, the 92nd and 93rd.

Though the 93rd moved around in the Pacific seeing very little action, the 92nd began fighting in Italy in July 1944. The Navy manned a sub-chaser and a destroyer escort, the *Mason*, with all-black crews. The all-black 761st Tank Battalion fought capably under Patton, at his request, from October 1944 on. The battalion captured 30 major towns in France, Belgium and Germany.

Heavy casualties in Europe forced the Army into unwilling integration in December 1944 and many blacks took demotions from supply outfits to transfer into the infantry units…4,562 volunteered within 2 months, showing, in the end, segregation couldn't put a stop to patriotism.

MYRA JEAN CLARK, parachute rigger third class, heads for the flight line at Floyd Bennett Field, New York City. World War II opened the doors for women to join all the military services in massive numbers.

TWO WACs CUT TRIM FIGURES. Women at left were right in fashion during the Victory Era, wearing their full-dress uniforms.

WAFS Barbara Jane Erickson (in cockpit) and Evelyn Sharp of the 6th Ferry Group at Long Beach, with a P-51A Mustang ready for delivery, early 1943.

National Archives

WASP P-47 PILOT below gets a final send-off from her Army instructor before climbing aboard the Thunderbolt warming up behind her. WASPs flew this heaviest of all single-engine fighters with a consistently outstanding safety and performance record, helping deliver aircraft from the factories at a record rate. The WASPs were finally disbanded in December 1944.

James Weir

ARMY NURSES above served on the island of Saipan during combat operations in 1944. Many women came under fire and died for their country, in spite of the official ban against placing them in harm's way. But if they were to do their jobs effectively, there was no option, and they performed with bravery and skill.

WACs STAND AT ATTENTION at the end of the war (right), along with a male officer. Many commanders were not very enthusiastic about bringing women into their domains, but wartime expediency won out and such men swallowed their pride. More than 17,000 WACs served overseas during the war, and by 1945 there were some 100,000 enlisted women and officers.

118566

A WAC IN TRAINING adjusts the radio antenna wire on a C-47 transport (left). Women were given responsibility for all jobs in the Army except those directly involved with combat. The results were dramatic and productivity increased, releasing men for more combat-related positions.

AIR BASE BRIEFING. A WAC operations specialist gives an Army pilot a preflight briefing at a Stateside air base below. Aircrews were delighted to find women in such positions...not only were their voices easier to understand, but maybe there was a date for Saturday night.

ZP·VL VD·JX   FB·SU   CG·LG   UY·PCE   WM·YZO   CANADIAN   STATE   TERMINAL   TERMINAL
NI·NC   LY·IG   FORECASTS   FORECASTS FORECAST'S FORECAST'S

WAVE RECRUITS (right) on their first day at Navy Midshipman's School, Northampton, Massachusetts State College, summer 1943. The Officer of the Watch (OW), inset below, checks them in. The Navy quickly filled its ranks with women, though equality of pay, among other things, did not get much attention from the men in command. It didn't matter a great deal to most of the WAVES who served...they were pioneers in so many ways, paving the way with sheer determination.

WASHING WAVES. The WAVES below scrub a Navy trainer at the naval air station in Jacksonville, Florida. Even the most boring of jobs were tackled with enthusiasm by women who were among the first to break in to what had been a male bastion. Those in naval aviation were among a very small band in a very small service, so the smile on this girl reflects her satisfaction with her job...or having cool water on bare feet during a hot Florida summer day.

WASPs IN TRAINING. Two women below prepare for a flight in a BT-13 basic trainer. The distinctive Santiago Blue uniforms and berets plus silver wings were worn with pride across the country. Men were often astonished to see women climbing out of the "hot ships" of the day.

DOING BANG-UP JOB. A member of the 92nd Division Engineers destroys an enemy mine at Viareggio, Italy, March 3, 1945. Like all black troops, this division had to fight entrenched discrimination in order to prove itself in World War II, not only in combat but in everyday duty. Usually, these divisions were given menial service tasks involved with supporting units in combat. Not until the last year of the war were black units put on the front lines to fight. In short order they proved to be as motivated and capable as any white outfit, leading to postwar integration of the military services.

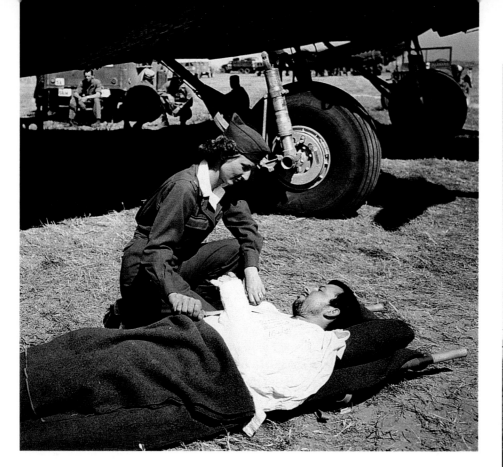

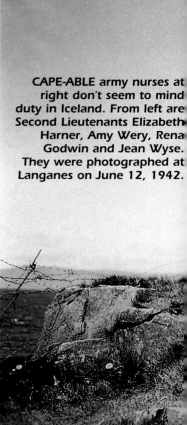

CAPE-ABLE army nurses at right don't seem to mind duty in Iceland. From left are Second Lieutenants Elizabeth Harner, Amy Wery, Rena Godwin and Jean Wyse. They were photographed at Langanes on June 12, 1942.

NIGHTINGALE IN BLUE. Army Air Forces Flight Nurse Lt. Frances Sale administers first aid to Pfc. Raymond Lobell.

Photos: National Archives

BLACK ENGINEERS of the 92nd Division begin sifting through the sand and rubble for mines at Viareggio, Italy. From left are Corporal Melvin Browder, Pfc. Lorenzo Cashe, Pfc. Parris Wade and Private Amish Fleming.

FLIGHT NURSE at left helps load a wounded soldier aboard a C-47 transport in the combat zone. In the Pacific, several nurses were captured by the Japanese and became POWs. They endured with determination and resolve in the face of an often ruthless enemy.

92ND DIVISION ENGINEERS below prowl the beach at Viareggio, Italy for mines in March 1945. Trying to clean up what the Germans had left behind was a dangerous and thankless job, but the all-black 92nd did it with efficiency.

Photos: National Archives

HERE COME THE WAVES! Recruits above are taking physical training at Navy Midshipman's School, Northampton, Massachusetts State College, summer 1943. The drills could build up to some strenuous exercise...just how strenuous depended on the DI (drill instructor). Some of the women DIs were reputed to be tougher than the men.

MODEL SHIP above has this WAC's attention during a visit with an old seafarer in England. The well-shined shoes she's wearing represent one of the more difficult transitions from a "civvy" to army personnel. Those stiff GI-issue shoes were known to create blisters, but once worn in were rugged and even comfortable. As tough as it was to wear them, most WACs agreed the experience was better than one's first set of high heels.

MAIL CALL. The WACs in England above take time to read mail from home. Women overseas quickly found themselves in a whole new world. Though exciting, the new surroundings did bring on longing for home. Mail from family and friends was coveted.

ANNA ROSENBERG (left) confers with a WAVE and WAC in her Washington, D.C. office. Responsible for much of the administration dealing with women entering the military services, Rosenberg had to report not only to her immediate superiors but to Eleanor Roosevelt, who took special interest in how the programs were progressing.

TUSKEGEE AIRMEN. Black Army Air Forces instructors, pilots and mechanics became so labeled because the Army segregated them from line units and sent them to Alabama's Tuskegee Army Air Field for training. Out of these pioneers came, at first, the 99th Fighter Squadron that entered combat in 1943 with "war-weary" P-40s. With three additional squadrons, they became the 332nd Fighter Group flying brand-new P-51 Mustangs, the finest fighter of the war. In spite of strong opposition from many in the Army chain of command, the "Red Tails" (named for their colorful fighters) ran up an outstanding combat record.

CHAPTER EIGHT

LIFE IN THE PACIFIC THEATER

American defeat and withdrawal pretty well describe the first 6 months of the Pacific war. Just hours after the Japanese attacked Pearl Harbor on December 7, 1941, they hit the Philippines, which fell in May 1942. By the following February, they had Java, then landed in New Guinea and the Solomons in preparation for an invasion of Australia.

The first hints of a reversal came in early May of 1943 when Japanese attempts to take Port Moresby, New Guinea were thwarted and the Battle of the Coral Sea was fought to a draw. That battle was a match between aircraft carriers.

As the Japanese advanced up the Philippines, they were opposed by an ill-prepared peacetime Army and five squadrons of obsolete P-35 and P-40 fighters. Not until late summer 1942 did Army pilots flying from Port Moresby start to seriously challenge their Japanese navy and army counterparts.

In September, a new fighter, the P-38, arrived. Among its pilots was Richard Bong, who would later become the American ace of aces with 40 kills.

Fought Through the Jungle

American Army troops slogged it out in New Guinea and in amphibious invasions with the Marines, while Army bombers attacked up the New Guinea coast.

Roving bands of American fighter planes continually harassed the Japanese. As 5th Air Force commander General George Kenney put it, "This means air control so supreme that the birds have to wear our air force insignia."

Air supremacy gave General Douglas MacArthur's island-hopping campaign the cover he needed to push toward the Philippines.

U.S. strategy established a string of land bases and overlapping zones of air control. MacArthur and Admiral William Halsey coordinated their campaigns to island-hop their way up the southwest and eastern Pacific.

The effort went so well the Solomons were secured and by October 1944, four U.S. Army divisions invaded the Philippines. Massive B-29 Superfortresses started flying from Saipan and Tinian in late 1944, laying all of Japan open to mass bombing.

Next Stop, Japan

As the enemy homeland was bombarded, U.S. officials laid plans for the invasion of Japan itself, which some strategists believed would result in a million casualties and draw the war out at least to the spring of 1946.

The vast Pacific, once a Japanese lake, had become one monumental staging base for American military power aimed directly at the Japanese home islands.

The B-29 was the single weapon most feared by the Japanese, and for good reason…as many as 800 could be launched at one time, and before the end, that aircraft alone dropped almost 170,000 tons of bombs.

The ultimate use of the superbomber came in August 1945, when it dropped atomic bombs on Hiroshima and Nagasaki, forcing immediate Japanese surrender.

A YOUNG RECRUIT gives a proper military salute to a 345th Bomb Group officer at Dulag, Leyte, 1944. The young local was one of many children befriended by Americans across the Philippines, bringing some much-needed humanity to a tough job.

George Fleury

BIG BUDDIES. Interned Japanese children on Saipan (left) had no qualms in making friends with Army Air Forces officers Bach, LaForge and Weir. Children were the most pitiful of war victims, even in this internment camp with relatively good care from the Americans.

SPOILS OF WAR. American servicemen at right look over a Japanese fighter Ki.61 (code-named Tony) just after moving in to a base formerly held by the enemy in Hollandia, New Guinea, May 1944. On the right is Thomas McGuire Jr., second highest ranking American ace of the war with 38 kills.

James Weir

PARACHUTE REPACKING was a critically important job in all aircraft units, and these men from the 24th Squadron, 6th Bomb Group on the island of Tinian are hard at it. The unit's B-29s were flying all the way to Japan and back and many crewmen had to use their parachutes.

BRIEFING

John Howett

James Weir

Wilbur Kuhn/ Mrs. Wilbur Kuhn

RAINBOW OVER SAIPAN. Beautiful view down the rows of 19th Squadron, 318th Fighter Group tents in 1944 was a brief respite from mud, heat, insects and enemy.

PINUPS were popular among GIs during the war. This road sign at Saidor, New Guinea in 1944 took advantage of that to put across a lifesaving message.

National Archives

Frederick Hill

FALLEN FOLIAGE. There wasn't much left after an intense battle in the Pacific. At times, entire islands would be left bare except for the mute testimony of what looked like bare logs stuck into the ground.

WALKING THE PLANKS. These pith-helmeted navy men are laying down pierced steel plank on a new bomber strip at Bougainville, a job that lasted from December 15 to 19, 1943. It wasn't an easy job, but was the only compromise between bare dirt and a paved runway. There wasn't enough time to build sophisticated facilities.

National Archives

Jack Cook

GOIN' TO THE CHAPEL. Palm-frond chapel at left with genuine native construction was erected by U.S. servicemen at Finsch-hafen, New Guinea. Chapels were very important to fighting men...there were no atheists in foxholes.

FILIPINO BOYS report for duty at the 345th Bomb Group camp at Dulag, Leyte. The headgear and emblems were given away without a qualm by men who enjoyed making these children part of their lives.

George Fleary

CAMOUFLAGE NETTING intertwined with local vines hides this B-24 Liberator from prying eyes in a revetment at Kualoa Strip on the east coast of Oahu, Hawaii, September 1943. After the Pearl Harbor attack, camouflage and disbursement became standard, though the likelihood of another Japanese attack became ever more remote as the war went on. These revetments were dug into rising ground.

George Fleary

WARTIME SYDNEY, Australia was a great spot for leave in the Pacific Theater…if you could get it. Martin Place (left) was bustling despite rationing and shortages.

LETTER HOME. American serviceman Clyde Barnett (below) takes some time to correspond in the alert shack at Strauss Field, 27 miles from Darwin, Australia, April 1942.

NOSED OVER. This 17th Pursuit Squadron P-35A inadvertently kissed the earth at Clark Field, Philippines in summer of 1941. Little did these men realize this tranquil area would soon become a bombed-out battlefield.

Fred Roberts/Bill Bartsch

BATTLEFIELD BLOOD BANK. The need for whole blood at the front lines was never anything but overwhelming, in every theater of war. Delivery by air was by far the most efficient, even in these relatively slow UC-64 Norseman utility transports. Since blood had to be kept cool, these canisters held dry ice.

MUD AHEAD. The 345th Bomb Group medical section reaches a relatively clear stretch of jungle road while making its way to a beach encampment at Dulag, Leyte, Philippines. Keeping up with the continual movements of an Army bomber unit was tough. The aircraft would be flown out to the next field in pursuit of the Japanese, but support crews and equipment had to be taken across land, then moved by ship to the next island. Once there, they had to slog their way through the jungle to the new base.

George Fleury

MOTOR POOL FRIEND. Filipino boy at left attached himself to the 17th Recon Squadron's mechanics during the unit's operations out of Leyte.

MONSOON MUD has mired this 17th Recon (Bomb) Squadron command car and its support trailers at Lingayen on the island of Leyte.

MEXICAN FIGHTER PILOTS are briefed by Captain Jesus Blanco, 201st Fighter Squadron, Mexican Air Force, at Clark Field, July 1945.

JUNGLE HEADQUARTERS of the 17th Recon Squadron at Binmale, Lingayen, Philippines. Shade kept the heat down...well, sometimes, anyway.

WAITING TO SHIP OUT of Hollandia, New Guinea for the Philippines, Sergeant Ed Barrett serves as a pillow for Corporal Jack Fruh. Both served in the 17th Recon Squadron's photo section, using airplanes with cameras.

HOUSE MOVERS. When the 345th Bomb Group moved to Clark Field, Philippines in June 1945, after over 3 years of Japanese domination, the men found they could buy ready-made houses and have them moved...by sheer manpower... straight into the new living area.

Maurice Epstein

FORDING THE RIVER on the way to Vigan, Luzon, 17th Recon Squadron photo section personnel found unique ways to deliver supplies to the Signal Corps in the Philippine hinterlands. Though World War II is remembered as a mechanized conflict, ancient methods of transportation often got the job done more efficiently.

Frederick Hill

A REAL MOUTHFUL. A can of pineapple was a rare treat for Sergeant Robert Casey (left) as he waited to ship out of Hollandia, New Guinea in October 1944. Red Cross girl above enjoys a picnic with servicemen at Mindoro, Philippines.

ENEMY AIRCRAFT TAIL provided a chance to parody the famous song about monkeys and Zamboanga, made famous by Wallace Beery in one of his 1930s movies.

MORET FIELD
ZAMBOANGA
ELEVATION 25 FEET

85ᵀᴴ AAF
WEATHER
STATION

-35

THEY HAVE NO TAILS
IN
ZAMBOANGA

Courtesy David Menard

Charles Van Bibben

SPIDER'S WEB, the name of the night fighter's club on Guadalcanal (shown at left in April 1944), was a play on the Black Widow airplane. Night fighter crews were proving a new form of warfare by flying aircraft that stalked their prey by radar. They flew P-61 Black Widows.

BOMB LOADING. Two armorers below slowly raise a 500-pound bomb up onto a P-38 Lightning using the small cranks fitted to the sides of the wing pylon.

Below and right: National Archives

SMOKE STACKS. The Marines at left are stacking 500-pound bombs at Kadena, Okinawa prior to bombing nearby Naha. Marine fighter pilots were only minutes from their targets, fighting an enemy just over the next ridge that was giving fits to their rifle-carrying buddies on the ground.

OKINAWA CONVOY. The 6th Marine Division moves through Okinawa on May 6, 1945. This island was nearly the last step before invading Japan.

WAR DOG SICK-BAY

SICK AS A DOG. This combat pooch is being treated by Pfc. Vincent Salvaggo and Corporal John Snowell on Guam, May 26, 1945. Dogs were useful in finding Japanese soldiers hiding on the island, particularly in caves.

COLD CANVAS. This navy base in the Aleutian Islands was little more than a tent city erected in March 1943. Trying to fight a war near the Arctic Circle was miserable ...for both sides. Later that year, the Japanese pulled out and called it quits.

PT ON THE PROWL. PT boat above patrols the Aleutians on November 20, 1943. There were seldom any Japanese targets to find.

A B-25 ARMORER heads out to his bomber in the Aleutians during summer (left). The matting on the ground was the only thing that kept aircraft flying off soft tundra in warm weather.

PBY ON PATROL. Navy patrol bomber crews contended with hours of boredom over the Aleutians, searching trackless spaces. This Catalina flying boat is doing just that in March 1943.

OUTDOOR MAINTENANCE at Adak, Aleutian Islands, 1942, was rough on everyone. Hands were cold and raw most of the time, but these Army aircraft needed continual attention to stay operational.

FIGHTER DROP TANKS sit ready for use at Adak, Aleutians. These auxiliary fuel tanks could be hung under a plane's wings in place of bombs to give greater range.

WHAT WINDS! These Army flyers are having a tough time just getting to the mess tent.

NISSEN HUTS provide shelter from the Iceland snow on July 1, 1943. This structure and its kin, the Quonset hut, probably housed more military personnel in World War II than anything, other than tents. Cold, uninsulated and drafty, they nevertheless kept the rain out and some of the warmth from a potbellied stove in.

National Archives

PET PARROT at Leyte (right) was a wild bird trained by this Army transport pilot in the Philippines—much to the respect of those around him.

HOME DELIVERY? Officers of the 77th Bomb Squadron (below) read a Sunday paper that somehow made it to Cold Bay, Alaska in late June 1942. Summer had come, just barely, to the Aleutians as the first Americans began to arrive to answer the Japanese invasion. These men flew many missions against an elusive enemy in their B-26 Marauders.

George Miltz

CHAPTER NINE

SERVING IN CHINA, BURMA, INDIA

The CBI Theater was by far the most difficult for the Allies to keep supplied after the Japanese cut off the only known route, the Burma Road.

With Allied forces active deep inside humid, jungle-thick mountain ranges, the only realistic alternative was to supply them by aerial transport. Thus, planes began flying across "the Hump", the Himalayan mountain ranges separating the Middle East from China.

Those who served here faced continual lack of proper food, shelter and other basic necessities, but fuel and ordnance became the overwhelming need. Transport pilots did battle with some of the world's worst weather to bring in badly needed supplies.

For the first year of the war, the only effective Allied striking force was General Claire Chennault's American Volunteer Group, the Flying Tigers, who were actually hired as civilians to fight for China.

Allies Turn the Tide

Up to 1944, Allied units were continually mauled by a Japanese army that understood jungle fighting better than any force in the world. With 100,000 troops, they marched for India, but determined resistance by outnumbered units held until the Japanese fell back to Burma, starving and in rags.

Major General Orde Wingate then led an airborne assault with 10,000 Southeast Asian commandos recruited by the British. Meanwhile, Merrill's Marauders fought with Chinese troops under General Vinegar Joe Stilwell on the other flank.

With much give-and-take, each side falling back then regaining ground, Allied forces made it to the Burma Road and retook Rangoon from Mandalay.

The disintegrating Japanese units ceased to be effective—except in southeast China, where the Japanese Army remained a powerful force.

Part of the reason lay in China's own civil war between Chiang Kai-shek and Mao Tse-tung, which drew resources from the combat zones. Right up until the surrender in September 1945, the Japanese were able to resist Allied efforts at pushing them out. This made aerial supply missions over the Hump all the more critical.

Followed the Aluminum Trail

The basic Hump route from Assam, India to Kunming, China took pilots over some of the most desolate terrain on the planet. When crews went down in the Himalayas, few ever came out. They nicknamed the route the "Aluminum Trail" for the 450 transport planes that went down, often used as gleaming navigation checkpoints.

The airlift began in April 1942. By March 1943, 2,278 tons went over the Hump, and by July 1944, the total was 18,975 tons. The record monthly total of 71,042 tons was flown in July 1945. As the war neared its end, around 650 planes flew the route every day. Total delivery by August 1945 came to 650,000 tons of everything from shoes to bombs to trucks to bulldozers.

Those who served in the CBI often felt forgotten by those at home. The Chinese did everything they could to make conditions better, but they had lived in basic poverty for so long there was not much they could really do.

Quarters were rarely well heated enough, and the summers never seemed to be anything but sweltering. When it rained, often in monsoon strength, the ground turned into an impossible gumbo, and when it was dry the dust would rise up several thousand feet, choking everything in sight. Americans in China, Burma and India faced many more enemies than the Japanese in the jungle.

ALLIES IN INDIA. American Serviceman Richard Clark posed with an Indian guard at the 12th Bomb Group base in Fenny, India. Supplied by the British Army, well-trained native soldiers manned most of the guard and anti-aircraft gun posts on the field...and got along well with the transient Americans.

Hank Redmond

NEW PALS. Serviceman Hank Redmond (right) made a little friend at Darjeeling, India, the heart of tea country. The children in this beautiful area took to American GIs and acted as local guides.

GAME OF CHANCE in Darjeeling (below) helped pass the time for these Americans far from home, a welcome diversion from combat duties.

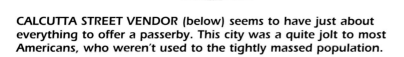

Hank Redmond

CALCUTTA STREET VENDOR (below) seems to have just about everything to offer a passerby. This city was a quite jolt to most Americans, who weren't used to the tightly massed population.

Hank Redmond

SHANGHAI STREET at left bustles with rickshaw traffic and peddlers carrying their goods for sale. The Chinese were hardworking people always on the move, whether tending their farms or carrying on commerce in the business district.

DOWNTOWN SHANGHAI discovered postwar re-emergence in September 1945. The Sun Department Store has a large picture of Chiang Kai-shek while victory is proclaimed in English on one of the large billboards.

Hank Redmond

Cal Bannon/Bill Bielauskas

FRESH MILK! Lieutenants Jim Moore and Richard Weber (above) enjoy their first taste of real "moo juice" in 9 months and drink as much as they can during a brief leave at Darjeeling, India. Good food and drink was hard to find in the combat zone, so soldiers on leave sought it fervently.

BURMESE BASKET CARRIER. American Cal Bannon (left) met this woman at Katha, Burma in March 1945. Foreign customs were often a puzzle to boys away from home for the first time...women who carried large loads on their heads were a source of wonderment.

INDIAN SOLDIERS man the anti-aircraft guns around the 12th Bomb Group base at Fenny, India. These men would often spot "Washing Machine Charlie" at night and start firing away. This single Japanese bomber's sole mission was to keep Americans awake at night, even though it did drop some bombs to little effect. Hank Redmond recalled, "We were never hit, but one small bomb, estimated to be a 25 pounder, did land about a half mile away once." Washing Machine Charlie's aircraft engines would change pitch, hence the nickname.

Hank Redmond

WATER IN CALCUTTA was always available, but no American ever dared drink it. To U.S. forces, the city's energy seemed to be directed toward nowhere in particular, and few people were at work—jobs were difficult to find for the millions roaming the streets.

AUSTRALIAN SOLDIERS below fish on a river in Monywa, Burma. Hank Redmond remembered, "Colonel Schmidt, the American liaison officer with the British 14th Army, had his bearers throw a hand grenade in the river, gather up the fish, then prepare us a delightful dinner of fish and rice curry cooked over an open fire."

THOMPSON, REYNOLDS AND McKENNA were part of Hank Redmond's original 12th Bomb Group B-25 crew during training at Columbia, South Carolina. Though split up, they served up in the same area flying combat on different aircraft.

YANKAI, CHINA (below) was a world away from most Americans in 1945. Rice planting and harvesting was nearly the sole occupation in this area, and war didn't seem to keep anyone from their tasks. Though a battle may have raged nearby, the primary concern of the locals was to acquire enough food for their families.

Carroll Barnwell

BACK TO LIFE. Shanghai was bustling at the end of the war in August 1945 (above). Rolling trolleys and busy people are in evidence everywhere. The rickshaw remained a popular form of transportation, particularly for visiting American servicemen and women who always seemed to be attracted to the experience.

Hank Redmond

CALCUTTA TROLLEY. This city remained one of the places where Americans could go for "R and R". When supplies had to be obtained, it was off to Calcutta, where you could make your shopping rounds on the reliable trolley—with a mile-long wish list given you by those staying behind.

TINY TOWER. American serviceman Sterling Reynolds struck this smiling pose (left) before the 490th Bomb Squadron's control tower at Fenny, India. The rickety construction was common to all buildings there, from personal "bashas" to official offices.

CAL-CUTTER. Street barber on the sidewalks of Calcutta has about the lowest overhead in the city. With no shop to care for, all he has to do is sweep the hair aside and sit his next customer down. Such scenes were a revelation for visiting Americans.

Left and below: Hank Redmond

ADDRESSING THE TROOPS below is Supreme Commander Admiral Lord Louis Mountbatten, Allied general over Southeast Asia. In Burma, he talks to the 1st Air Commando Group with Colonel Phil Cochran standing in the background, fourth from the right.

R.T. Smith

Fred Poats

Carroll Barnwell

AN AIRFIELD BUILT BY HAND. Chinese laborers above flatten the runway at Liuchow, China with nothing more than manpower. All the rubble to be ground and pressed for a hard landing surface was carried in by people, dumped on the ground, then rolled to a firm, smooth finish. The Chinese were remarkable in what they could do in a short time...and they did it all across China at dozens of airfields and military installations.

THE SUN DEPARTMENT STORE in Shanghai (below) carries a prominent reminder to the locals that Chiang is the ruler of China. The streets were always teeming with people and business, rarely slowed down by the war. This photo is a close-up of larger shot on page 143.

Harold Cohen

B-25 PILOT William Tascher appears pretty proud of his Wabash Cannonball in Yankai, China, 1945. This model of the Mitchell bomber carried a 75mm artillery piece in the lower left section of the nose.

GRAND HOTEL

George Saylor/Bill Bielauskas

Hank Redmond

DISNEY CHARACTER. Walt's stylized tiger with wings became the symbol of the Flying Tigers. At right, R.T. Smith stands in front of one of the decals supplied by Disney Studios free of charge...they were applied on rough paint, then shellacked.

MILK RUN (far right) was a B-25 with the 12th Bomb Group at Fenny, India. Nose art shows mama and her pups. The last little guy in line has fallen on his face trying to keep up. Nose art was a badge of honor, and crews worked hard to pay for it, sometimes bartering with artists to have these images painted.

GRAND ACCOMMODATIONS. The Grand Hotel in Calcutta sure beat jungle living. Officers on leave often made this building headquarters, enjoying clean sheets, fresh food and card games.

BURMESE WOMEN wait for their rice allotment at Momauk airstrip. Laborers were supplied with rice... the war brought consistent employment to areas where there were no jobs outside meager farming.

Cal Bannon/Bill Bielauskas

Hank Redmond

WHO NEEDS AIR-CONDITIONING? Pilot Bob Younger flies a 12th Bomb Group B-25 on a training mission over India. Bob has found a way to beat the oppressive heat and humidity …he's wearing only a parachute and has the window all the way open! This broke every regulation in the book, but no one that far away from home really cared about regulations. Quite often the crews would bring along drinks, which chilled nicely above 10,000 feet.

CHAPTER TEN

WE'RE COMING HOME!

If there was a universal American sentiment about World War II, it boiled down to this: Let's get it over with and go home.

Patriotism certainly had its heyday during those years, but the overpowering desire to end the war as soon as possible permeated every home, factory, ship, tent, unit and squadron. When the war finally ended, it unleashed a flood of raw emotion that will most likely never be repeated again.

Victory in Europe came on May 7, 1945, when the Germans surrendered at 2:41 a.m.

The rejoicing then was staggering, but when officials announced victory over Japan the following August 14, the nation went wild. Millions of Americans took to the streets at home, while men and women overseas whooped and hollered. They'd be coming home at last.

Actually getting on a ship to come home was another matter entirely. With millions of soldiers and sailors overseas, a point system was set up for rotation home. It was based on time served away, and the more points you had, the closer to the front of the line you'd get.

Cruises Were Cramped

Human cargo had to be packed into every available space on ships and planes heading back to the good ol' U.S.A. Many Army Air Forces crews were lucky enough to fly their own bombers and transports home, but most returned in crammed ships, such as the *Queen Elizabeth*, which made numerous runs from England to New York, each time with 14,000 aboard.

Navy personnel had it made, since most sailors were serving on a ship that simply waited for its orders to turn around and head back for home port.

Unfortunately, rotating millions upon millions home ended up taking years. Thousands of disgruntled GIs waited in backwaters from Germany to Okinawa well into 1946 and 1947, while still more served in the occupation forces. There wasn't really much to do without an enemy to fight, other than shuffle papers and stand guard duty.

But impatient as they might have been, these men and women were the lucky ones...some 300,000 Americans wouldn't come home at all, missing, lost at sea or buried in foreign fields.

Traveled by Train, Plane, Thumb

When they finally reached American shores, GIs wasted no time finding the fastest way home. If bus terminals, train stations or airports were jammed with waiting lines, they hitchhiked, walking between lifts to reduce every foot between them and home.

Back home, family and friends eagerly awaited them, praying for the quick return of the loved ones they hadn't seen for months or years. Some men came home to toddlers they'd only met through V-Mail photographs. Others returned to parents who'd reluctantly let a high school boy go to war. They came home older, tired and ready for peace.

Home front families knew difficulties, too. They'd emerged from 4 long years of rationing, having worked as Red Cross volunteers, war bond sellers, air raid wardens and factory personnel.

They'd also witnessed Europe's devastation through newsreels and letters. Their understanding helped support soldiers through the difficult readjustment period. Getting back to normal wasn't always easy.

America was still here, though, and that was the most important matter of all. U.S. soldiers didn't have to return to help rebuild a country devastated by bombs or a land scarred by trenches and shelling. They came back to a free land anxious to greet them, thank them and give them the lives they left to help people in places far away from home.

CHRISTMAS CRUISE. Lieutenant Fred Poats spends Christmas Day 1945 in the Pacific aboard the SS Alderamin, happy to be going home after a long tour in China. Deck accommodations weren't luxurious, but Fred didn't care as long as the ship kept heading east. China had been an adventure for Fred, standing him in good stead for a future as an agricultural engineer.

CLOGGED TRAFFIC near Bolzano, Italy (left), just after the German surrender, is a study in contrasts. Germans, Italians and Americans are mixed together in this convoy trying to get back home.

V-E DAY SMILES. Staff Sergeant Kermit Riem, Technical Sergeant Roger Fraleigh and Sergeant Robert Sand (below) look pleased when they struck this pose in Wormingford, England. The announcement of Germany's surrender in May 1945 was met initially more with relief than joy. It was over, at last, and almost everyone would start rotating home to get on with their lives.

PLEASED IN PARIS. WACs below are getting some essential information from the local gendarme as people pour out of buildings and start looking for friends and neighbors to help celebrate V-E day. Paris was one long shout of joy and triumph after 5 years of war on French soil.

VE DAY today
MAY 8 '45

Robert Frizzoli/K.I. Kalley

John Meyers

National Archives

WINSTON CHURCHILL (center, with British general officers) was a brilliant spokesman and architect of Allied victory. Tenacious and unrelenting in his quest for complete victory over Germany, then Japan, he had the ability to cut through detail to the heart of a matter. He often exasperated Roosevelt, who nonetheless admired him, and he didn't get along with Stalin, though both forged a mutual, at times begrudging, respect.

JUBILANT THRONG. V-E Day in Paris brought thousands of people into the streets to celebrate together, French and non-French alike. Any form of traffic, other than pedestrian, was out of luck...every intersection was blocked with yelling, joyous Parisians letting out years of pent-up emotion. At long last, Paris was again the city of love and light.

Mark Brown/USAFA

AUGSBURG, GERMANY was half rubble just after the surrender in 1945 when Alexander Sloan of the 1066th Signal Company took the shot above. The center of Messerschmitt production, the town was subject to repeated bombing attacks, as were most cities with factories.

REFINERY IN RUINS. One of the concrete blast walls around an oil refinery storage tank at Misburg, near Hannover, Germany, stands in mute testimony to Allied bombing. Three American Army officers survey the facility at left.

JAPANESE SURRENDER. On August 19, 1945, two bombers, painted white with green crosses to identify them as nonbelligerent, brought the initial peace delegation to the island of Ie Shima. The Japanese emissaries quickly boarded American C-54 transports to continue their trip to Manila, where they would meet with General Douglas MacArthur to arrange for a formal surrender ceremony. The sight of the bomber at right drew quite a crowd—a trip home couldn't be far away now.

Frederick Hill

IKE SPEAKS. Allied Supreme Commander General Dwight Eisenhower and Deputy Supreme Commander Air Chief Marshal Arthur Tedder (left) just after Ike's Victory in Europe speech, May 7, 1945. As the two men most responsible for the cooperative Allied effort in Europe, Eisenhower and Tedder were intelligent soldiers who believed fervently that cooperation between the U.S. and Britain was the single necessity for victory.

National Archives

STATESIDE, HERE WE COME! Personnel of the 406th Fighter Group, after a long, hard slog giving air cover to the Allied armies from D-Day 'til surrender, board a C-47 at Nordholz, Germany for the first rotation home, September 1945. This poor old "Gooney Bird", as the aircraft was nicknamed, is much the worse for wear after a long war. Most service personnel did not get to fly out...or at least no farther than the French coast to board a ship for the long voyage home.

Stanley Wyglendowski

SHIPPIN' OUT. The General E.T. Collins is ready to leave India for the States with combat cargo personnel. It took 64 days to sail home from Asia. While that was no picnic, who cared? It sure beat combat. The worst thing was just how many people the brass could cram on a ship this big. There was barely room to turn around, much less spend any time alone. Below decks, the heat and sweltering had to be experienced to be believed. Did anyone volunteer to get off? Not on your life!

George Saylor/Bill Bielauskas

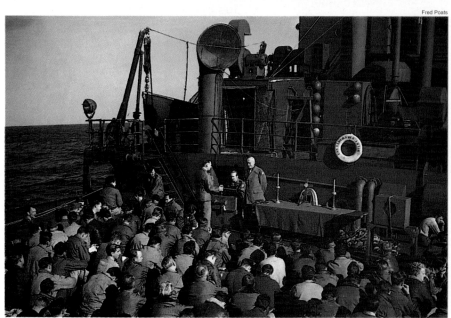

Fred Poats

VICTORY JAM. Men of the 71st Recon Group listen to an impromptu jam session on deck of the SS Cape Victory (above) while heading home from Manila to Seattle. Any form of entertainment was welcome...if there were some talented musicians among the group, so much the better. The deck was also an ideal spot to hang out laundry.

SHIPBOARD SERVICE. The men at right attended Christmas service in 1945 aboard the SS Alderamin. The ship crossed the International Date Line the same day. Most were very thankful for surviving the war ...church attendance, even on the deck of a ship, wasn't much of a problem for the chaplains coming home with their men.

Frederick Hill

Stanley Wyglendowski

John Worth

DOGS ON DECK? As much as it was frowned upon, most men tried to bring their pets back, even if they had to smuggle them aboard. This 406th Fighter Group officer doesn't seem to be having a bit of trouble walking his dogs on the Victory Ship Madawaska as it heads across the Atlantic for America.

Page 160-161 photo: National Archives

FIRST GLIMPSE OF HOME. When ships pulled into ports across the U.S., signs were strung on everything to make the boys feel welcome. This elevating bridge on the West Coast was a perfect signboard as ships passed beneath it.

AMERICAN SOIL! Members of the 345th Bomb Group, the Air Apaches, step off their C-54 at Hamilton Field, California on November 17, 1945, their first time home since leaving for the Pacific. Maury Eppstein turned around and took this shot after being away for 30 months and 17 days. Hamilton was just north of San Francisco, one of the greatest liberty towns in the country. That night the entire bunch were either out on the town or working their way home.

HIS MAJESTY'S SHIP QUEEN MARY anchors in New York Harbor on June 10, 1945 with a full load of American troops coming home from Europe. For men and women who'd been away for so long in foreign surroundings, there were few sights to compare with the New York City skyline and the Statue of Liberty. Prewar luxury liners like the Queen Mary had been pressed into continual service shuttling military personnel back and forth between America and England. Every cabin was jammed to fit as many as possible aboard, so much so that many chose to sleep above deck in the open air.

IKE SAYS "ATTABOY". General Dwight Eisenhower (left) addresses the 101st Airborne Division at Mourmelon, France on March 1, 1945 during the award of a Presidential Unit Citation for the division's actions during the D-Day invasion. The 101st's paratroops had jumped behind enemy lines the night before the invasion to cut off German lines of communication, coming under heavy fire, but they held their ground. In just a few months they would be in Berlin as a part of the American occupation, then the men would rotate home, at last.

National Archives

James Kunkle

ARMY TUGBOAT CREW decorated their humble vessel (below), turning it into one of the first "Welcome Home" signs vets would see, as they did here from the Westminster Victory pulling into New York Harbor from Europe in 1946. Home at last!

FAMILIAR AND FRIENDLY SKYSCRAPERS jut out from the New York City skyline (above) as a homebound troop ship rounds the tip of Manhattan for the harbor. Lining the rails, most everyone seemed glued to the sight, unwilling to look away as if it were a dream and might disappear.

Stanley Wyglendowski